THE JUDAICA IMPRINT
FOR THOUGHTFUL PEOPLE

"Do you think that only people cry?"

THE
SHAAR
PRESS

RABBI NACHMAN SELTZER

HEAVEN'S TEARS

Sima Halberstam Preiser's
journey to life

Published by **SHAAR PRESS**
Distributed by MESORAH PUBLICATIONS, LTD.
4401 Second Avenue / Brooklyn, N.Y 11232 / (718) 921-9000

Distributed in Israel by SIFRIATI / A. GITLER
6 Hayarkon Street / Bnei Brak 51127, Israel

Distributed in Europe by LEHMANNS
Unit E, Viking Business Park, Rolling Mill Road / Jarrow, Tyne and Wear, NE32 3DP/ England

Distributed in Australia and New Zealand by GOLDS WORLD OF JUDAICA
3-13 William Street / Balaclava, Melbourne 3183 / Victoria Australia

Distributed in South Africa by KOLLEL BOOKSHOP
Northfield Centre / 17 Northfield Avenue / Glenhazel 2192, Johannesburg, South Africa

ISBN 10: 1-42261-438-7 / ISBN 13: 978-1-4226-1438-9

Printed in the United States of America by Noble Book Press Corp.
Custom bound by Sefercraft, Inc. / 4401 Second Avenue / Brooklyn N.Y. 11232

*T*his book is dedicated

in loving memory of
my grandfather, parents, brothers, sisters, other relatives,
and the over six million kedoshim who were killed in the
Holocaust.

HaRav Yitzchok Yeshaya ben HaRav Chaim Hy"d
HaRav Yaakov Tzvi ben HaRav Yitzchok Yeshaya Hy"d
HaRabbanis Chaya Sara bas HaRav Elazar Hy"d
Chaim ben HaRav Yaakov Tzvi Hy"d
Malka bas HaRav Yaakov Tzvi Hy"d
Rivka Henna bas HaRav Yaakov Tzvi Hy"d
Yehoshua Shalom ben HaRav Yaakov Tzvi Hy"d
Baruch ben HaRav Yaakov Tzvi Hy"d

And to my partner in life, my dear husband,
Yaakov ben Nechemia HaKohen, z"l.

━━━◆◆◆━━━

And to my sister Devora, and my brothers
Usher and Chaskel, who have always been with me,
even when we were physically apart.

And last, but not least, to my wonderful children, grand-
children, and great-grandchildren who mean the world to me,
and who are the living testimony and continuing links in my
history: Yonatan Zvi & Sandy, Uriel Ze'ev & Sharon, Haya
Malka & Avrohom, Michelle (Michal Rivka), Lauren (Rachel
Chana), Tova Rivka & Simcha & Roi & Hallel, Raquel Miriam &
Yehoshua & Batya Leah & Yosef Chaim & Shira & Yaakov Zvi,
Chaim Nechemia, Eliyahu Zvi & Michal, Yehoshua Shalom &
Dorit, Sara Malka, Esti Nechama, Netanel Baruch, Adina Leah,
Ari (Yehuda Ari), Chaim Yitzchok Yeshaya, Rivka Sara, and
Shea (Yehoshua Shalom).

Sima Preiser (nee Halberstam)

TABLE OF CONTENTS

AMERICA

HOW THIS BOOK CAME TO BE

I KNOW THAT MOST PEOPLE SKIP THE DEDICATION or preface portion of a book, but I think you will get more out of my mother's Holocaust memoirs if you pay attention to this section, too. I am the oldest of my mother's three children, and there was five years between each of us. Therefore, there is a significant difference between what each of us heard from my mother, and when we heard it, as we were growing up.

We were lucky enough to grow up in a house full of love, between our mother and father and between our parents and us. My parents were heroes to me and I admired them both. Each of them had a unique story.

Because I was the oldest, my mother's wartime memories were still very fresh when I was a child. I still remember the nightmares she would have, and my father cautioning me not to ask too many probing questions. My mother rarely spoke of her experiences during the Holocaust, but it was a presence that was always felt in our home. Most of the stories of her experiences were told to me by my father rather than my mother. He also instilled in me a strong hatred of the Nazis and a refusal to ever forgive or forget their atrocities.

As time passed and my siblings were born, my mother was able to talk more and more about her life and the Holocaust. It was not until I'd already left home that she opened up even further, and so it came about that my brother and sister actually heard her stories firsthand before I ever did. However, I still remember my mother's screams and night terrors, which had thankfully subsided by the time my brother and sister were growing up.

One of the things that always occurred to me over the years, as I heard more and more about my parents' lives, was that their stories would make for great reading. However, as is usually the case, I never really acted on the thought, other than to ask them more questions about their lives. The years passed until, in 2009, my father, z''l, who was living in Petach Tikvah, Israel, passed away after about three years of illness. I had never even had the chance to discuss a book about his life with him. He was such a modest man that he probably would not even have understood why his life's story was worth recording. With my father's passing still fresh in my mind, I was even more motivated to record my mother's story while we still could.

It was right about then that my siblings, quite independently of my own thoughts, suggested that we should get my mother's life's story down on paper. At the same time, my mother met two women, Shira Leibowitz Schmidt and Jessica Setbon, who write articles and stories in Israel in both Hebrew and English. They initially met my mother at an event at Kiryat Sanz and were immediately interested in her story. They sat with her several times and wrote a wonderful article for the family, dealing with my mother's arrival on the

Lower East Side of New York after the war and her early life in Israel after making *aliyah*. These two women were instrumental in encouraging our mother to begin telling her story for publication. They also provided research into various background aspects of our mother's family and her story.

The book idea was starting to come together, and while at first we thought of writing something strictly for ourselves, our children, and grandchildren, the possibility of creating something that might also be of interest to others gradually took root. My sister had read several books by Rabbi Nachman Seltzer, and enjoyed his writing. The fact that he was a published author and could therefore possibly reach a wider audience for the book was also a consideration.

Since he lives in Israel, as do my mother and brother, it was decided that my brother would approach him and see if he was interested in writing the book for us. He agreed to meet with my mother. At the same time, we wanted to see how she felt about opening up to him and telling him of her experiences. Since you are reading this book, it obviously went very well—and the result is this book.

It is a bittersweet moment. I wish my father could have lived long enough to see this book, and long enough to provide us with enough material to write a book about him. Even more, I wish that my mother hadn't had such a story to tell, that her life could have been a quiet and uneventful one in which she grew older with all of her beloved family around her. That all six million Jews could have lived their lives to the fullest.

But since they were not given that choice, we should never forget and never let it happen again. I hope that this book, which was initially conceived so that our own family would never forget, will be a source of inspiration for you and your family as well.

Yonatan Zvi Preiser

PROLOGUE

DO YOU THINK THAT ONLY PEOPLE CRY?

Do you think the Gate of Tears only grants entrance to our tears, but doesn't have any of its own? I'm here to tell you that Heaven's Gate produces tears as well.

That the Gate of Tears knows how to cry, just as we do.

———◆———

Zeide Shaya'le was standing in the room he used as a study. Outside, the Germans were closing in on us, entrapping us in their snare. Every week, more streets in the ghetto were cordoned off by the evil men in their dreaded uniforms and emptied of their Jews. Our world had shrunk to a miniature universe. The majority of the ghetto's Jewish inhabitants had been shot to death or rounded up.

Terrible, terrible decrees. And yet, Zeide still needed a study, because he needed to learn. It was his greatest love.

He was truly old by then. Stooped, bent over, a shadow of his former self. Yet from his eyes flashed a fire that reminded me of the man he'd been in his younger years. That fire was clear evidence that the Zeide I'd always known and loved was still there.

He looked at me questioningly.

"Simchah'le?" (The name he always called me.) There was a tremor in his voice.

"Yes, Zeide."

"Did the Belzer Rebbe leave yet?"

He must have known that the Belzer Rebbe was long gone. Maybe he'd forgotten. He was very old.

"Yes, Zeide. The Belzer Rebbe was smuggled out of Bochnia a long time ago."

The room was still, the air redolent with the scent of tea and *sefarim, sefarim, sefarim*, the Jewish holy books that he loved with all his heart. Even now several were open on the table.

And then Zeide Shaya'le stepped out of himself.

"You will go in peace—*b'shalom*," he told me, his beautiful, timeless eyes full of tears. "You, Simchah'le, will save yourself. You will be saved. You will live."

Everything he said sounded like a prophecy of old, and Zeide himself seemed like an ancient *navi*. The next words he uttered shocked me to my core.

"Your mother and your father — They will not survive —"

I wanted to pull back. I didn't want to hear these awful predictions. But I felt a compulsion to continue questioning him, pressing him about what the future held.

"And you, Zeide? Will you live?"

My voice was tremulous, the voice of a little child seeking reassurance from someone she trusts and receiving none, because there is no reassurance to give.

Zeide raised his finger and spoke again in his elderly, wavering voice. "*Nein, mein kind* (No, my child)."

"Only I will survive?" (*Ribbono shel Olam*—how horrible a fate! To be the sole survivor of such an illustrious family!)

"No, you will not be alone. But the majority will not survive."

We stood together, and yet alone. Zeide Shaya'le and I, his beloved granddaughter. The smell of a wax candle filled the air as it slowly suffocated to death in the airless chamber.

I began to cry. Zeide Shaya'le was shedding tears, too. It was the only time in my life that I ever saw my Zeide cry.

We began moving toward the window. He was talking to me and shuffling over to the window at the same time—the one that looked out at the ghetto partition. Zeide moved the paper curtain aside just a tiny bit.

It was pouring outside.

The rain was coming down as if someone had opened a gigantic faucet and was letting it run until the world below drowned in the flood. The water hit our window-pane, streaming downward with incredible force. Far off in the distance, thunder boomed. A jagged edge of lightning slashed the bloated sky with intense savagery. We stood there, crying together, and Zeide said, "*Zeist, mein kind, inz veinin. In himmel veint mein mit inz.*" ("See, my child, we're crying. In Heaven they're crying along with us.")

It was the most terrifying moment in my entire life.

Just then, my father entered the room and said, "Sima, you have to leave now. *Schnell*. Quickly. Right away!" There was an urgency in his voice that could mean only one thing. Germans.

I took my Zeide's hand in mine and kissed him goodbye. Then I left the room, shoulders heaving, despair in my heart.

How we loved that man! Such a wonderful, loving person.

Do you think that only we cry—that the Heavens don't know how to shed a tear?

I can assure you that they do. I've seen those tears. Seen them up close.

I left him then. It was time to fulfill my Zeide's promise. I would survive. There could be no doubting Zeide Shaya'le. He knew. He always knew.

POLAND
THE EARLY YEARS

CHAPTER ONE

I GREW UP IN A RELATIVELY LARGE FAMILY. WE were five boys and four girls. Today, there are four of us left: my older sister Devora, my two youngest brothers, Usher and Chaskel Duvid (David), and myself. That's all.

Usher was a twin. Baruch, his twin, did not survive. Nobody knows for sure how Baruch perished. Nothing is documented. But we've heard personal accounts of those final days of *Gehinnom*. Stories of those last moments in the ghetto when Zeide Shaya'le and Tatte were taken away. There was a child with them. We assume it was Baruch.

Chaskel Duvid was the youngest child in our family.

And I? I was a middle child, mischievous and lively.

At the war's end, we four were the sole survivors of what had been a beautiful family. The Halberstams. Jewish royalty, one of the illustrious Chassidic families in Poland.

The rest of my siblings have their own stories. They all perished, each in a different way. We know how some of them died, but others remain stories that are only known in heaven.

———»·•·«———

I was born en route from Sucha to Cracow, on a train. How's that for making an original entrance into this world? My father, Rav Yaakov Tzvi, was the Rav in Sucha and the surrounding villages. We lived in our innocent little village, with our fruit trees and our animals, until late 1938 or early 1939.

Sucha. A small town. Bigger than a village, smaller than a city. There were many Chassidim residing in our town, adherents of the Sanzer and Bobover rebbes who, like my father, were all members of the Halberstam Chassidic dynasty. And the scenery was straight out of a fairy tale. Bubbling brooks and sapphire lakes whose cool waters were just perfect for children. There was a forest surrounding the town: endless trees standing tall and self-important, like an army of soldiers that could do anything it set its mind to. And then there were the mountains. We could see their slopes and peaks from our streets and homes. This was countryside at its best.

Our town was located not far from a famous vacation/ skiing resort, and I have no doubt that Sucha could have been developed into a resort village as well. The weather was glorious for much of the year and it was an absolutely enchanting place to live.

———»·•·«———

Our family did not make a point of celebrating birthdays. Consequently, I do not really know how old I am. One woman who lived in Sucha insisted that I was the same age as her daughter, and since *she* was born in 1930 there was really no question. But one of my relatives claimed that she was speaking nonsense.

"You were born on a train," he said. "In fact, I recall the exact day. I'll never forget the excitement."

"Please tell me everything you know," I begged him.

"Well," he acquiesced, "your mother was very sick when she was expecting you. She went to a top specialist, who diagnosed her with heart complications and ordered her to have the baby in Cracow, where the hospitals were far more advanced than in the villages.

"And so, off they went.

"However, your mother went into labor in the middle of the journey. The train was forced to stop at a tiny station right outside a little village, where you were born. The joy and excitement in Sucha were palpable. Everyone smiled and joked. They said things like, 'She was born on a train, she'll be traveling for the rest of her life.'

"And that's how I know that your exact birthday was in 1932, and not in 1930."

He spoke with assurance. His story was very convincing.

And yet, there were still other conflicting accounts.

Recently, a cousin from Canada, a grandchild of Rav Bentzion Bobover (her mother was Rav Bentzion's daughter and her father was my father's brother), told me that *I* was born in Adar of 1931, while *she* was born in the summer of the same year.

So there's a three-way controversy about my age, which doesn't really matter in the long run anyway. The ironic thing is that I truly did spend my life traveling all over the world, just as had been predicted for the child who was born on a train.

———◦———

My oldest sister had been named Fraydel, after my mother's mother. Fraydel, unfortunately, passed away in infancy. When I was born they wanted to name me after her, but were faced with indecision because one doesn't normal-ly name a baby after someone who passed away at a young age. My parents finally arrived at what they considered an acceptable solution.

I had been born in the month of Adar—a Purim baby. A child born on one of the most joyful days of the Jewish year, in the happy month of Adar. Zeide Shaya'le was consulted, and he had two things to say.

First, it was brought down in the name of my great-grandfather, the Divrei Chaim, that the name Simchah works equally well for boys and girls. It's even spelled the same way.

And, second, Simchah and Fraydel mean the same thing. Joy. Happiness.

So they named me Simchah. Sadly, my name did not bring me much joy. In fact, I suffered a great deal because of that name.

Let me explain. Growing up, I had plenty of chores to do in the house, and additional tasks were added later on, when we moved to Cracow. For example, I was the one who was always sent to bring the candles into the *Beis Midrash* on *Motza'ei Shabbos* so Zeide Shaya'le could make *Havdalah*. This meant entering the men's section and bringing the lit candles to my grandfather.

How the young boys laughed at me.

"Your name is Simchah," they'd scoff at me. "Just like a boy."

"You have braids. They look like *peyos*. Just like a boy."

"And you're always in the men's section. Just like a boy!"

"Are you sure you aren't really a boy?"

In the end, the powers-that-be allowed me to rename myself Sima. But my Zeide would always refer to me as Simchah'le.

———⇒•⇐———

Today's kids have lots of toys. Maybe a few toys too many. My childhood was a happy one. I enjoyed myself to no end. I had many friends, many relatives, many wonderful siblings. . . but toys? There were very few to speak of.

I had a doll.

It had been given to me as a present; I can't recall by whom. I treasured that doll. I loved her with all my heart. I'll never forget the moment when Tatte took my doll and stuck pins in her face so that she shouldn't be considered an object of *avodah zarah*. I never removed those pins. Tatte had put them in and I would not take them out. And those pins made no difference to the love I felt for that doll.

She had beautiful hair, she wore the outfit of a little Polish peasant girl, and I adored her in my uncomplicated way. But even mothering my doll paled in comparison to games of the imagination we played. Having so little in the way of material possessions meant that we knew how to use our minds, that we learned how to discover our creative intellect.

We played store.

One girl worked in the store. She stood behind the counter. She was the storekeeper.

The rest of us were the customers. And we knew how to shop. We were experts when it came to haggling over prices. We knew how to examine merchandise to make sure it was fresh. We were familiar with all the tricks. Stones we gathered from the ground became rice and flour in large sacks, while other stones became potatoes and onions, cabbage and sugar. These were games rich in mind development, colorful and full of detail, because *we* added the color and supplied the details.

Life could have been perfect, but it never was, because the gentiles in Poland and Galicia regarded Jew-baiting as a form of sport and our non-Jewish neighbors in Sucha were no different. It didn't matter that we were the children of the Rabbiner. We played with our Jewish friends and never crossed the line to the other side. It just wasn't worth it.

I had lots of friends. The *shochet* had a number of daughters close in age to my sisters and me. The *melamed* had a daughter as well. We spent our days in a childish world of innocent imagination. I loved those friends dearly. The *melamed's* daughter survived until the Bochnia period of our life. The other girls didn't even make it that far. I remember every single one of them as if we parted yesterday.

We were so happy, despite possessing almost nothing in the way of material playthings. Our minds were more than enough.

The gentiles in Sucha got around by horse and buggy. That was the preferred method of transportation in the Galicia of my youth. The buggies were not well constructed, but at least they weren't subjected to constant wear and tear the way their tires were. Wagon owners had to change the tires on a regular basis. And tire-changing meant that we children were in for an unexpected largesse. We took possession of any abandoned tire. We held races: who could keep their tire up and running the longest, with the merest touch of a stick. We ran and laughed and enjoyed ourselves immensely—with nothing more than a discarded tire.

A ball. A used tire. A jump rope and, of course, my pin-faced doll. That was the extent of my toy collection. When I lived in Cracow I struck it rich, because some of the young men who studied in my Zeide's *Beis Midrash* built a carriage for my doll. The carriage didn't have wheels, but that was no problem for a child whose imagination worked overtime, every waking minute of every day.

We had very few personal belongings, and yet I daresay we were a lot happier than many kids of today who have so much more.

———

Sucha was surrounded by beautiful shady woods that beckoned us into their leafy embrace. Our mothers would take us out to gather blueberries and raspberries for pies and preserves. We'd frolic on the riverbank, playing our make-believe games and eating our sandwiches and enjoying our uncomplicated lives. But all was not quiet.There was also a lime pit in Sucha.

The lime pit was infamous. It was a very dangerous place for anyone, and especially for children. You'd think that the Polish government would realize that an open lime pit should warrant a gate around its perimeter, but no—the pit was left open, the powerful stench of lime wafting into the distance. The knowledge was handed down from child to child: here lies danger. This was a place to stay away from.

But I had a little game that I played whenever I got bored. I loved to hide.

I was four or five years old. A tiny girl, so thin that I could slip into almost any space and the grownups couldn't follow. Well, one day I disappeared, and the entire town joined together for the search. The fear was that I had some-how forgotten how dangerous the lime pit was and had managed to get stuck inside.

The truth, however, was far more prosaic.

There was a long porch that circled the outside of our house back in Sucha. A marvelous place to play and romp. Beneath that porch was a cordoned-off area where my mother raised chickens before each *Yom Tov* (holiday) and baby goats before *Pesach* (Passover). It was caged in and airy. The birds were there only some of the time. The rest of the time it was clean and empty—the perfect place for a mischievous kid who loved to hide. That's where I was, tak-ing it easy in the rectangular space under the porch, while the entire town searched and called my name, growing more and more agitated as time passed and I was still not found.

I had devised a safety net. Whenever I sneaked away and found somewhere to hide, I'd make sure to take one of my brothers along, thereby ensuring that I wasn't the only one to blame when the good times were up and the hard hand of Mother came down on us.

On that particular occasion, while the entire town anxiously searched in every place they could think of, it was my brother Baruch whom I'd convinced to come along for the ride. He complained and wanted to leave, instinctively knowing that we were going to get into a heap of trouble when our parents finally managed to track us down. But I worked very hard at keeping him there beside me, telling him all sorts of stories, cajoling him to remain, and even warning him that Mama and Tatte were going to be very angry with him when he came out and that it would be a lot safer for him if he were discovered together with me. Eventually he fell asleep, and so did I. Both of us drifted into a deep, restful slumber, while the shouts and calls of the neighbors passed us by

I don't know who found us in the end, but I'm sure that I was treated to a lesson calculated to ensure that I never forgot what had occurred on that fateful day, and how worried they'd all been. That might be why I still recall this particular incident, even though so many years have passed since then.

Another time, I'd been playing in the room where my father taught his students, when the group arrived to learn. Maybe I wasn't supposed to be there, because I quickly squeezed beneath the closest couch and hid, waiting to see if someone would find me. Of course, the end of the story was quite the usual: I fell asleep. As I always did.

My independent nature was coming to the fore even back then, when I was still little more than a baby. And that nature would come in very useful later on, when the time came to take a stand.

————◦————

Nine children is a houseful of kids, yet I do not recall fighting with my siblings. That's not to say that they enjoyed having me around all the time. My older sisters, in particular, had to cope with my hanging around, because after me came four boys. As much fun as they were, I was still a girl who looked up to my sisters and wanted to emulate them. They, however, relished their freedom from their precocious younger siblings and were not above using a hint of subterfuge to get rid of me from time to time.

One Shabbos afternoon, my sisters felt the need to escape.

They did not yell at me.

They did not hurt my feelings.

They simply escorted me into the kitchen, where they showed me a simple trick they were sure I would love to know.

If I mixed sugar, cocoa, and a little water — viola! I had a piece of chocolate! This was a wonderful experiment, and I got very busy making my own delicious creation, while they escaped to their friends without my tagging along.

And they did it without making me feel bad at all.

————◦————

Shea was about eighteen months younger than I was. We were a team and we did everything together. There was nothing Shea wouldn't do for me, and vice versa. He was the sweetest of the sweet.

And the twins were such special boys.

That's the way it was in our home. The older children took care of the younger ones, with my older sisters cutting shapes out of napkins for me, Shea playing games with the twins, Shea and I getting into all sorts of mischief together — one big, very happy family.

— ⋄ —

Sucha was a small town. Not much happened there on a daily basis. The big excitement happened once a week, when the market opened up for business.

Reb Abba'le was our neighbor, a diminutive man and a *"zeeseh mentsch"* (a sweet gentleman). His wife sold lace in the marketplace. The lace came to them on a regular basis from relatives overseas, which meant that they had no overhead. Every bit of money they made was profit. She had a technical problem: her Polish wasn't very good. Still, she did her best.

I used to help her with the Polish.

One time, after she'd closed on a nice deal, she gave me a beautiful gift that I never forgot. Reb Abba'le and his family moved to Cracow at around the same time we did. Sweet Reb Abba'le was one of the first Jews to be killed by the Germans upon their arrival in Cracow.

He was just a simple Jew of prewar Galicia, but people like him were worth their weight in gold.

— ⋄ —

Sucha was a town that took pride in doing *mitzvos* (good deeds). The community built a *cheder* above the *shul*, along with a few rooms where passing visitors could stay. Those rooms were always full.

My mother, Chaya Sara, was a real Rebbetzin. She was descended from Kaminka, an illustrious dynasty in its own right. Her great-grandfather was Rav Sholom Kaminka. My great-grandfather, the Divrei Chaim, and Rav Sholom Kaminka had been *chavrusos* in their youth, and they'd remained the closest of friends. They even married about the same time. There was a tremendous love between them, and they promised each other that they would one day make a match between their two families. That Sanz and Kaminka dynasties would remain intertwined, like the most impressive vines of the finest grapes.

Rav Sholom passed away at a very young age. He left one son, Rav Shea.

Rav Shea's son became a son-in-law of the Divrei Chaim. That was my mother's father, HaRav Luzer Rosenfeld, the *Dayan* of Oshpitzin. Which meant that my mother was descended on one side from the Kaminka dynasty, and from the Divrei Chaim of Sanz on the other side. From what I understand, Kaminka had a reputation of being even more stringent with their spiritual obligations than Sanz was. She was a queen and scion of two royal families. And yet, she cared about everyone who lived in our town as if they were part of her own family.

There was a couple who had a son who was very sick. (It may have been tuberculosis, which was prevalent in those days.) My mother made sure that this family received a cooked meal, delivered straight to their home, every day of the week. Families took turns cooking for them, and that meal was delivered without fail.

I was about five years old, too little to carry everything myself, but not too little to help. I would trot off to visit whoever was supposed to prepare the meal for the next day and remind them to make it a really good one. Sometimes people took offense at my forthright manner and would scold me for being so disrespectful. Afterward, my mother would ask me why they'd thrown me out of their homes, and I'd be forced to explain exactly what I had said and the tone I'd used that upset them so. Then my mother would scold me as well, for upsetting the women who had graciously volunteered to make such beautiful meals.

Not that it did much good. I was a free spirit and couldn't be tamed, no matter what anyone said.

———

Zeide Shaya'le was the most important figure in our lives by far. Youngest son of Rav Chaim Halberstam, the Divrei Chaim of Sanz (so called, as was the custom, after the title of his book for which he was known and the town in which he lived), Zeide Shaya'le was the patriarch of the family. Respected and loved by all, his advice was frequently requested and always heeded. His words were cherished.

We were frequent visitors in Zeide's home. The trip from Sucha to Cracow was one that we made all the time. And I visited Cracow and Zeide's home even more often than my siblings, due to an ear infection that never really managed to heal properly. Cracow, as the nearest big city, had the best doctors in the area. Every time my ears needed prodding by the men in the white coats, I found myself visiting *"der Zeide"* and spending a lot of time with him as well. I considered myself lucky

I had an aunt in Cracow who had only one son and wasn't overly busy. She was always happy to take me to the doctor. On other visits I stayed at Zeide's house by myself. Consequently, we became very close. Whenever I talk about my Zeide, even now, seventy years later, tears come to my eyes. I feel his presence in the room, I see his smiling face and I hear his voice, tinged with his ever-present good humor. For me, my Zeide lives on.

———

Zeide Shaya'le lived in a very large building in Cracow. The style was reminiscent of Spanish architecture. These buildings are built with inner courtyards where the family can gather to relax on a shady veranda. In Cracow, the buildings were erected in a similar way, but much larger. Zeide's building had a giant rounded entrance that allowed its tenants access to a huge enclosed area where children played their games and teenagers sat immersed in lively conversation. There were a few more buildings "standing guard" at the corners of the gigantic courtyard, whose brick walls gave us the feeling of playing in the secluded environment of our own little world.

Zeide's building was located on a very Jewish street which included a Talmud Torah and a number of *shuls*. I don't think any gentiles lived in his building. It was an island of *Klal Yisrael* situated in the middle of a sea of non-Jews.

Cracow is a very Catholic city and there are churches everywhere. There was even a seminary for the priesthood close to Zeide's home. We could see the *galuchim* in their black robes, coming and going with somber expressions, and we knew that we wanted nothing to do with those people. This was something we assimilated almost by osmosis. Stay away from the priests. They've inflicted too much damage on the Jews of Poland and Galicia over the generations. Watching them strut through the ancient city streets was the closest we came to any of them.

And Cracow was where Zeide Shaya'le had a small *Beis Midrash* (school). It was a warm place where a *Yid* could come to hear a bit of Torah from Zeide and recharge his spiritual batteries under the benevolent gaze of the Divrei Chaim's youngest son.

This was the core of our family's existence.

———⟫•⟪———

My Zeide's name was HaRav Yitzchak Yeshaya Halberstam, also known as Reb Shaya'le Tchetchov. As previously mentioned, he was the youngest son of Rav Chaim

Sanzer. Zeide was called after Tchetchov, a small city near Sanz where he'd served as Rav before moving to Cracow.

Rav Chaim Sanzer, the Divrei Chaim, had had three wives.

His first wife gave birth to seven children. After she passed away, the Divrei Chaim married her sister, who was an extremely sickly woman. She passed away not long after the marriage, at which point he married again. I am a descendant of the Divrei Chaim through both his first and third wives.

The Divrei Chaim's third marriage blessed him with another seven children, two of whom were boys. The older of the two was fondly referred to by our family as "*der feter* (the uncle) Reb Shulem Leizer." He was a very special man who was also the father-in-law of Rav Bentzion Bobover. Our family is very closely related to the Bobover Halberstams. In fact, my mother, who is descended from the *Yid* or Yehudi Hakadosh, was Rav Benzion's first cousin on both sides. Her mother, who married into the Oshpitzin family, was a daughter of the Divrei Chaim and my Zeide's sister. Thus my mother was my Zeide's niece and my father's first cousin.

My mother was Rav Bentzion's cousin on her father's side as well, because Rav Bentzion was her grandmother's great-nephew. We were related many times over and this meant that our family and the Bobover Halberstams were extremely close. Just as the royal houses of Europe were interrelated, so were the great Chassidic dynasties.

My Zeide was twelve years old when his father, the Divrei Chaim, passed away.[1]

The fact that my Zeide and his brother Reb Shulem Leizer were the Divrei Chaim's youngest sons meant that

---

1. (Author's note: At the time of this writing, there are fourteen great-grandchildren of the Divrei Chaim still alive.)

they developed a very close relationship with their father. There is something special about the way a father relates to his youngest children as we see from the relationship of Yaakov Avinu with his sons Yosef and Binyamin. Thus, my Zeide enjoyed an unparalleled connection with one of the greatest *tzaddikim* of his generation.

After the Divrei Chaim was *niftar*, his two oldest sons adopted the two youngest sons. They brought the boys into their homes and taught them Torah along with their own children. That is why many of the descendants of the Sanzer family bear the name Chaskel Duvid: those were the names of the two oldest sons. One was Chaskel, the other Duvid. Because of the age gap between them, they were like parents to their younger siblings, who showed them *hakaras hatov* by naming an entire generation of illustrious *tzaddikim* after the two of them.

My Zeide Reb Shaya'le was also married three times. In those days, many women passed away during childbirth or from illness. He had two girls and a boy with his first wife, who was related to the Belzer and Apter dynasties as well. Their son was Rav Chaim Tchetchov, who later settled in New York and brought us over after the war. Their daughters married into Chassidishe royalty; one of them was the mother of the future Chernobler Rebbe.

A memory stands out in my mind.

I was a little girl, and I needed shoes. Little girls back then wore out their shoes just as they do today. Maybe even more quickly, because they walked a lot more. We were already living in Cracow by then, and a shoemaker had his establishment on our corner.

I saw a perfect pair of shoes in his window. They were every girl's dream, patent leather with a design. There was even a bow attached to the front. They were just the kind of shoes I would be proud to wear. And I really needed shoes.

I went to Mama.

"Mama, I need new shoes, and I saw the most wonderful pair in the store on the corner —"

"*Zeeskeit*," Mama replied, "ask Zeide Shaya'le for money."

A little child is not shy. And certainly not one as precocious as myself. I had no problem asking Zeide for money. I presented myself to my grandfather, told him that I needed shoes, and explained that I had fallen in love with a pair of shoes at the corner shoemaker's. Zeide reached into his pocket and handed me the money. I had to wait to buy the shoes, because Mama had to take me and she was very busy.

One day, Zeide Shaya'le called me over to his side and gently asked me if I had already purchased the shoes.

"No," I answered truthfully. "My mother hasn't found the time to take me yet."

Zeide nodded thoughtfully to himself, and shared the following story with me.

"I had a little sister," *Der* Zeide began his tale. "And there came a time when she needed shoes, just like you. Her shoes were ragged and worn out and they hurt her feet. My mother instructed her to go ask her father for money. (Some things never change!) So my sweet little sister went off to her father, the Divrei Chaim, to ask for money. The Divrei Chaim reached into his pocket and gave her enough money to buy a new pair of shoes.

"Now, the Divrei Chaim was a famous European rebbe, which meant that there was a constant chain of people coming to his door begging for assistance, both the financial and moral kind. Not long after my little sister received the money she intended to use to buy shoes, the Divrei Chaim called her to his side and wanted to know whether she had purchased the shoes.

"My little sister," Zeide said, "was just as truthful a little girl as you are. She told her father that her mother hadn't had a chance to take her for shoes just yet.

"The Divrei Chaim asked his daughter to bring him back the money that he'd so generously given her."

"And then he explained why he needed the money.

"'Did you see the woman sitting in the waiting room?' he asked his daughter. She nodded. 'That woman has a little girl whose every dress is torn and ragged, and who owns a pair of shoes with more holes than leather. She came to me, begging me to help her. That's why I asked you to bring back the money. So we can give it to a sweet little girl who has holes in her shoes.'

"My sister looked up at her holy father and said, 'But I also have holes in my shoes, Tatte!'

"And do you know what *der Tatte* told her?" My grandfather looked down at me with his kind, wise eyes.

"What, Zeide?" I asked breathlessly, drawn into the story.

"He said, 'But you are my daughter. Everyone will play with you, even if your dress is worn out or your shoes have holes in them. But this other girl isn't as lucky. Who will play with her if her clothing looks like that? Won't you bring me the money so we can do a *chesed* (a charitable deed) for her?'

"And my sister ran to her mother and asked her for the money.

"She didn't buy new shoes for herself. Because she was the daughter of the Divrei Chaim and everyone would play with her, even if she never had new shoes.

"My Simchah'le," Zeide Shaya'le said to me, "a Mama came to me just before to pour out her heart. She, too, has a little girl just like you. And this little girl has no coat and shoes that are falling apart. Would you like to be like my sister, and give me back the money so that the little girl's Mama can buy what she needs?"

He looked at me lovingly.

"And you know that everyone will play with you and love you even if you don't have new shoes right now—because you're my Simchah'le!"

It was a hard decision, but not that hard. To have *der Zeide* compare me to his sister. . . that wasn't an opportunity that came along every day. I ran to get the money. And I was happy to hand it over, even if it meant that the patent-leather shoes in the corner window would remain a dream. Who cared about patent leather and bows when Zeide Shaya'le was actually comparing me to his own sister?

Not I.

I never got those shoes. But *der Zeide* had compared me to his sister. In my eyes, that was a fair trade.

CHAPTER TWO

O UR FAMILY'S IMPORTANCE IN THE CHASSIDIC world of Europe was in no small part due to our being descendants of the Divrei Chaim. When I was small I heard many wonderful tales about the Divrei Chaim: the miracles attributed to him, his strength of character, and the love he had for every Jew. I have forgotten most of them. But there are several that simply refuse to leave my mind and that I would like to pass on to my children, grandchildren, great-grandchildren, and generations yet to come. I want them to know from whom we are descended.

One story was the tale of the apple.

A poor woman came to my great-grandfather, the Divrei Chaim, on a Shabbos eve, crying bitterly.

"What's the matter?" he asked.

It took the woman time to get herself under control, and he waited patiently. It seemed that she was a fruit peddler. In better times, she'd always managed to earn a respectable living from the fruit she sold in the marketplace. But this year's crop of fruit was of an inferior quality, and nobody was buying. She was desperate. She needed money for Shabbos. What was she supposed to do?

The Divrei Chaim calmed the distraught woman.

"Don't worry. Everything will be all right." Then he motioned to his *gabbai* to bring him his *bekishe*. The rebbe was going out.

They left the house: the Divrei Chaim, the *gabbai,* and the still-weeping woman. My great-grandfather turned to the woman and asked her, "Where do you sell your fruit?" And he accompanied her to her stand.

He saw a pile of unappealing fruit. Rotting apples. Moldy pears. The woman hadn't been joking. Who would even consider buying such merchandise?

The Divrei Chaim was undeterred.

He approached the fruit cart and immediately found his rhythm.

"*Yidden!*" he called out. "*Heilige Yidden*—an apple! Buy an apple *l'chavod* Shabbos."

The holy rebbe had become a peddler!

As he spoke, he picked up one of the apples from the top of the pile, cradling it in his hands, displaying it to the shoppers in the marketplace.

His voice rose and fell. The holy voice of the Sanzer Rav.

"An apple, an apple for Shabbos. *Yidden, heilige Yidden,* buy an apple for Shabbos!"

When the Jews in the marketplace saw the Divrei Chaim selling those apples, there was a mighty rush toward the cart. Within minutes, every last piece of fruit was gone.

The Sanzer Rebbe's love for every Jew had shone forth once again. The woman returned home from the market, her pockets laden with money to buy food for Shabbos.

———✦———

Zeide Shaya'le loved hearing stories about his father, the Divrei Chaim. I was very attuned to the things that made my Zeide happy and knew about this love. Zeide had a *Beis Midrash* (a school) in the house where his Chassidim used to gather.

Enter little Sima. I knew how to talk to people. I'd tug at the men's long coats, and when they looked down at the bundle of energy who was intruding on their conversation I'd demand that they tell me a story about *"der Sanzer Zeide."* Some of the Chassidim were elderly themselves, and they remembered a great many incidents involving my holy ancestors.

"Tell me a story. Tell me a story," I'd beg.

And they would.

As soon as my Zeide entered the room, I'd turn around and rush toward him, plowing my way through the group surrounding him on every side. They all knew me and smiled at the little imp who was running through their legs, crowing, "Zeide, Zeide, I have a story for you about the Sanzer Zeide!"

And my Zeide would stop everything.

"Sha!" he'd command the assembled. *"Mir vellen yehtz heren a maaseh fun dem Sanzer Zeide* (We will now hear a story about the Sanzer Zeide.)" And I would tell the story, and he would smile. He knew all the stories. They were like old friends.

As a reward, I'd receive a coin of the lowest denomination, or maybe just a pat on the cheek. But it was worth it, just to see those loving eyes light up when I spoke, repeating the stories about where we came from, of the miracles *der Zeide* had wrought, of his kindness and devotion to his Chassidim and his connection with the *Ribbono shel Olam.*

When the Divrei Chaim first came to reside in the city of Sanz, he was invited, along with his entire family, to live in the home of a community leader, Reb Yidel Hakohen Hollander. Reb Yidel paid for everything in the kindest, most gracious way. He undertook all the expense of hosting the Divrei Chaim on his capable shoulders, and honored him as much as he was able. In short, the Halberstam family was very comfortable at the Hollander home. But Reb Yidel had a question that wouldn't leave his mind. It was a very simple question, but it gave him no rest.

Simply speaking, Reb Yidel wanted to know whether the Divrei Chaim was capable of showing favoritism to someone that he knew or with whom he was friends. Since the Divrei Chaim had been designated to don the mantle of spiritual leader of Sanz, Reb Yidel wanted to be sure that he was worthy of the role. And what better candidate to test this question than himself, the benefactor and supporter who'd brought him to Sanz and had supported him so benevolently and generously?

So Reb Yidel decided to perform a test. A simple test that would prove the matter, one way or the other.

For his ploy, Reb Yidel needed the assistance of a friend, who gladly participated in the scheme. The basic idea was as follows.

The friend would come complaining to the Divrei Chaim in great agitation, claiming that Reb Yidel owed him a large sum of money and that he was refusing to pay his debt. Would the Divrei Chaim please summon Reb Yidel to a *din Torah*?

Of course the Divrei Chaim would. There was no question.

The Divrei Chaim wasted no time. He summoned his designated messenger with alacrity and requested that he write up a personal order from the Rav, demanding that

Reb Yidel appear before the *Beis Din* for a *din Torah* at once.

Reb Yidel read the paper, and replied in a manner indicating downright disdain for the Divrei Chaim and his official position as rabbi of Sanz.

"I am a very busy and important man," Reb Yidel stated haughtily. "I don't even have the time to reply to the summons."

His reply was contemptuous and brazen, and the messenger was extremely taken aback at the lack of *derech eretz* Reb Yidel had exhibited

But it wasn't his job to judge or make decisions. He had one job: to relay Reb Yidel's response to the Rav; which he did.

The Divrei Chaim took no notice of his patron's bizarre response. He told the messenger to return to Reb Yidel forthwith and tell him, in no uncertain terms, that he was to report to the *Beis Din* at the appointed time.

The messenger did his job.

Reb Yidel looked the messenger in the eye and uttered further extremely shocking words. "I am very busy. I don't think that's a secret. Why do you persist in bothering me?" His tone was scathing—the opposite of what is expected of one of the pillars of the Sanzer community.

"I have neither the time nor the inclination to drop everything and come running to the Rav for a *din Torah* right now," he continued in scathing tones, "If — *if* — it should happen that I find the time to come at some point in the future, then I will do so. But right now, it's not going to happen! Please tell the Rav not to bother me with this any longer."

Unspoken was the following message to the Divrei Chaim: "Who do you think you are? Don't you know how important I am? Don't you know that *I* brought you to this town?"

The Divrei Chaim heard the messenger and instructed him to return to Reb Yidel and warn him that unless he arrived promptly at the *Beis Din*, he, the Rav, would be forced to take serious steps against him. Translation of "serious steps" was usually *cheirem*.

Hearing this, Reb Yidel knew beyond a shadow of a doubt that the Divrei Chaim was the real thing. Sanz was extremely lucky to have him as their Rav. Then and there, he dropped the entire charade. The next moment he could be seen running down the street to the Divrei Chaim, where he related the entire story: how it had all been a ploy, a plot, so he would know beyond a shadow of a doubt whether the Divrei Chaim had the backbone to stand up to whomever he might need to.

Reb Yidel purchased and furnished a truly magnificent apartment for the Divrei Chaim. The Halberstams resided there until the Neugroschl family, affluent Sanzer Chassidim from Austria, decided that the time had come to build a very large, prominent house and *Beis Midrash* for the Divrei Chaim, his family, and the many Chassidim who came from near and far to spend time with their illustrious spiritual guide whenever they could.

The Divrei Chaim had a *minhag* to deliver a *derashah* every year on Shavuos. This was a complex *pilpul*, designed to make his listeners ponder and reflect deeply into the topic he was analyzing. One year, as he was concluding his *derashah*, the Divrei Chaim uttered a cryptic remark which nobody comprehended.

"Yossel Ropper paid noteworthy attention to the *derashah*," he said, "and understood every word."

This comment was puzzling. So what if Yossel Ropper paid attention, and so what if he understood every word?

But once you knew that Yossel Ropper had been an *am ha'aretz*, it became difficult to grasp how he, of all people, was able to understand every word. And to make the question even greater, Yossel was not even among the living any longer! He had passed on to the *Olam HaEmes* years earlier. What was going on here?

The Divrei Chaim did not allow his audience to ponder this mystery for long. All listened attentively as their Rav related a personal story.

"When I arrived in Sanz," the Divrei Chaim began, "the leading scholars of the town were waiting for me. The great *lamdanim*, those with sharp proofs and clear minds, those who had memorized all the commentaries, those who knew every Shach and Taz by heart. Everyone was there. They had all arrived to greet their new rabbi. To sing songs of welcome to their new leader.

"The second I alighted from the wagon, the entire cadre of Sanzer *talmidei chachamim* converged upon me with fire in their eyes. I knew what they wanted. They were determined to engage their new Rav in a *lomdish* discussion, to catch a glimpse of the depths of wisdom to which he could aspire. They crowded around me in a rush of raised voices and undulating thumbs, their faces excited and eager, their minds racing with every unanswered question that plagued them.

"In the midst of all the roaring confusion, a slight figure shyly approached and, whispering in my ear, told me that he had something extremely important, even urgent, to discuss with me in a nearby room.

"Something about him impressed me, and I gently disengaged myself from the adoring crowd. I followed this man, whom I'd never met before, into a side room where this special individual had prepared a wonderful meal for me.

"'I know how difficult traveling is, and the Rav has just

come a long way. Please partake of the meal I've prepared and relax a little before facing the crowd again.'

"I followed his good advice.

"Now, I know that you all recall Yossel Ropper as a simple Jew who couldn't read a *pasuk* in *Chumash* and was certainly not familiar with the intricacies of a page of Gemara. And yet, I've just announced that Yossel heard every single word and, even more importantly, understood everything he heard.

"How is that possible?

"The answer," explained the Divrei Chaim "lies in the fact that Yossel was so careful to do true, genuine *chesed*. He brought me back to life when I was exhausted, when my spirits were down after a long tiring trip. And that is why," the Rav concluded, "even though Yossel was a simple man in this world, he was given the opportunity and the reward of comprehending every word of the *derashah* today!"

———※◆※———

There was another famous tale told about my *elter Zeide,* the Divrei Chaim—a story I loved. It showed his marvelous understanding of human nature and his keen acumen.

A woman arrived at my great-grandfather's court. Her face was streaked with tears and her shoulders slumped in anguish. She'd had a terrible argument with her husband. It was not the first time. But she hadn't dreamt that it would be the last time, either. The Divrei Chaim wanted to know what her husband had said.

"He told me he was leaving, and that this time he wasn't coming back. But I didn't believe him. He'd made similar threats in the past and always returned."

"And?" prompted the rebbe.

"He hasn't come back. It's been a long time. It looks like this time he's staying away for good! And now I'm an *agunah*."

"Did you write to his relatives? Did you ask them if they know of his whereabouts?"

"Almost none of his relatives are willing to take the time to respond. They probably feel that he's better off without me, and don't want me to know where he's hiding! A few of them have written back that they don't know where he is. Obviously, he's cut off all ties with his family, to ensure that nobody tells me where to look for him."

The Divrei Chaim handed her some money.

"I want you to go to a certain village," he instructed her, telling her the name of the place. "When you arrive, comb the streets, look through the marketplace, meet the people, visit the *shul*. And wherever you go and whomever you meet, ask them if they know your husband."

She followed his instructions to the letter.

And there, in one of the village's *shuls*, she found him. Sitting with a *Tehillim* by the far wall, next to the oven, swaying and praying, and taken completely by surprise when he realized that she'd managed to track him down.

In the end, he had to give her a *get*.

How had the Divrei Chaim known exactly where to send her? Nobody knew. All concurred that it must have been a *mofeis*, and that the Divrei Chaim had *ruach hakodesh*.

———◆———

Another story about the Divrei Chaim goes as follows:

There was once a Sanzer Chassid who was forced to leave his hometown and move far away, to the town of Bad Neuheim in Germany. The Chassid was not happy about this development, knowing as he did that Germany was full of Jews who were much more progressive in their thinking than in Galicia. But his dire financial situation left him with no other choice.

The Chassid did his best to make a life for himself in his

new city. Because a Chassid needs a *shul* in which to *daven* and learn, and because there was no *shtiebel* for him to frequent, he began attending communal prayers at the main *shul* in town.

The *gabbaim* seated him next to a fine householder, an affluent individual who had nothing to say to the Chassid at all. In fact, not only did he have nothing to say to him, he barely even spared him a glance. After all, the Chassid was an *"Ost Jude"* (a Jew from Eastern Europe) while his neighbor was a modern, German man of the world. He had neither the time nor the inclination to associate with someone like the Chassid. After all, he was a successful investor and financial consultant, and who was the Chassid? Just another penniless, old-fashioned Jew from the East. And so, they ignored each other in the most polite fashion imaginable.

One day, the Chassid noticed that his neighbor did not appear to be doing so well. He looked run down and beaten, as if his entire world had collapsed around his shoulders. The Chassid felt sympathy for the man and, despite the German's insistence on maintaining a chilly distance, he asked him if everything was all right.

The German stiffly replied that all was well. His tone implied that the Sanzer Chassid should stay out of his life. But the German began looking worse and worse. He, who used to take such care and pride in his appearance, had let himself go completely. Gone was the proud posture, the stiff upper lip, forward-jutting jaw. Eventually, the Chassid couldn't bear it any longer. He cornered the man after *shul* one day and asked him again whether all was well with him.

The German studied him for a minute, clearly debating whether he could trust him with his problems. Finally, he said to the Chassid, "Do you really want to know what's bothering me? Do you truly care?"

"I really do," the Chassid assured him, earnestness

pouring from every pore, kindness radiating from him and embracing the German unreservedly.

"Well, then, please come to my office, where we can talk undisturbed in peace and quiet."

The Sanzer *Yid* needed no further invitation. He knew that the German must be experiencing major difficulties, and he wanted to help. They arranged a meeting and the Sanzer *Yid* made sure to arrive promptly, knowing the importance Germans attributed to punctuality. There the Chassid began to skillfully question his host, and within five minutes the German was weeping like a baby.

"What's wrong, my friend?"

"It's my business."

"Tell me more."

"This is the way it works," began the red-eyed businessman. "People invested money with me over a period of many years, and when they needed a very large sum of money—for example, to marry off a child—I provided it with no fuss. In the meantime, I invested the money in all manner of business enterprises, where it always did extremely well. Recently however, my luck has turned, and quite a few of my businesses have collapsed. I have no way to repay all the people the money I owe them."

Their eyes met. Sadly, the German said, "I don't want to say this, but it appears to me that suicide may be my sole option at this point. At least then I will die with my pride still intact."

"*Chas v'shalom!*" the Chassid screamed at his new friend, the echo of his voice reverberating throughout the room. "That's the worst thing you can do! You, who certainly believe in *HaKadosh Baruch Hu*, knows that a person must never give up hope. That even if a sharp sword is raised above a Jew's neck, he should never stop believing in *Hashem*'s salvation!"

"But what on earth am I supposed to do?!"

"I, myself, cannot help you," the Chassid told his new-found friend. "However, my rebbe, the Divrei Chaim of Sanz in Galicia, is one of the greatest *tzaddikim* (righteous men) of our generation. I have no doubt that he can help you."

"What should I do? Should I write him a letter asking him for a loan to cover my debt?"

"I don't know if he can lend you the money, but I do know that if you write the rebbe a letter describing your situation, he will find a way to assist you. I am completely sure about this."

The German took his advice. He penned a letter to the Divrei Chaim in which he described his desperate situation in detail. He was truly at the lowest ebb in his life and his feelings screamed forth from the lines he had written. He sent the letter off in the post and waited for a miracle.

Every day is an eternity for a man who is contemplating suicide, but at least he had stopped talking about that as an option. He'd sent his *tzaros* over to the Divrei Chaim, and was now awaiting his reply. And it was not long in coming.

The envelope was impressively bulky.

There was a letter inside, penned by the *tzaddik* himself.

"Do not despair. Not even in the most desperate of moments. A *Yid* must never lose his *emunah* in the *Ribbono shel Olam*."

There was a sum of money in the envelope as well. A very large sum of money. The German's heart leaped with joy.

"I am enclosing enough money for you start over," the Divrei Chaim wrote. "*B'ezras Hashem*, you will be successful and you will repay this loan to me at the proper time."

The businessman wanted to sing, he wanted to dance. His heart floated on a cloud of exultation. He was saved! His reputation had been salvaged. Using the money the Divrei

Chaim had sent him, the German went back into business like a whirlwind, conquering everything he touched. It didn't take him long to revert back to where he'd been before, sitting once again on top of the wheel of fortune.

One night, the German had a dream.

He dreamt of an old man with fiery eyes and a distinguished demeanor, who informed him in no uncertain terms that he owed him money. The German memorized every detail of the old man's appearance and went to pay a visit to the Sanzer Chassid as soon as it was late enough in the morning to do so.

The Chassid listened to every word.

"Describe the old man to me, please."

"I will try my best."

The German had a good memory. The more he talked, the more excited the Chassid became. Finally he could hold back no longer.

"You're describing the Divrei Chaim," he cried wonderingly. "The holy *tzaddik* came to you in a dream! *Ashrecha!* How fortunate you are! And yet," he continued, almost speaking to himself, "what are you going to do? How are you going to fulfill his orders? He is demanding repayment of the loan—but he is no longer alive to accept it!"

The German businessman was a loss.

He wanted to repay the sum he owed the *tzaddik* more than anything. He had the means to do so easily, as his business was flourishing. Yet the Divrei Chaim was no longer alive to take the money back.

The Chassid was equally bewildered.

The German carried on with his life. His business kept growing by leaps and bounds. Soon Bad Neuheim wasn't big enough for him any longer. He relocated to Frankfurt, where he quickly managed to cement his reputation as a keen man of business whose touch turned everything to gold.

One night, the Divrei Chaim appeared to him for the second time.

The German was ecstatic even in his sleep. Now he would finally find out how to repay the loan which was weighing on him so heavily.

"My son, Shalom Elazar, is about to make a *chasunah* (wedding)," the Divrei Chaim informed the man whose life he'd saved. "He has no money. I want you to find him and give him the sum I loaned you. This is how I want you to repay the loan."

Then the Divrei Chaim disappeared.

———»·•·«———

The German jumped out of bed the next morning, eager to carry out the *tzaddik's* bidding. He was in a very uplifted mood. Here was his chance to repay the goodness that had come his way—that had literally saved his life.

Soon enough he was standing at the train station: destination Bad Neuheim, home of the Chassid who had taken a moment to befriend a man he didn't know and who, at first, had treated him with cool disdain. And who, despite the German's cold and haughty behavior, had managed to save his life.

"I had another dream last night."

"Tell me, my friend. Tell me!"

Excitedly, the businessman repeated every detail of the dream, concluding with a request that the Chassid tell him where to find Rav Shalom Elazar.

"He lives in Hungary. That I know. Other than that, I'm not sure. The first thing to do is travel to Budapest. I have no doubt that the *Yidden* there will know."

Thanking his dear friend, the German took the next train to Budapest, where he asked around for the whereabouts of his benefactor's son. It wasn't long before he learned that

Rav Shalom Elazar resided in a town called Ratzferd.

He felt relieved as the train carried him into what he hoped would be the final leg of his journey. Ratzferd. Home of the Divrei Chaim's son, the holy Rav Shalom Elazar Halberstam. He had been waiting to repay this debt for quite some time now. The money felt as if it were burning a hole in his pocket.

He stopped a Jew in the street.

"Excuse me? Could you please tell me where Rabbiner Halberstam lives?"

The Jew gave him precise directions.

Finally, he found himself standing in front of the Divrei Chaim's son, the young man who was engaged to be married. A tremendous *talmid chacham*. A *tzaddik*. A beautiful *Yid* with a glowing countenance.

Rav Shalom Elazar looked at the German Jew, trying to figure out why he had come to see him.

"Is the Rabbiner celebrating a wedding soon, by any chance?"

Rav Shalom Elazar inclined his head.

"Do you have the means to pay for the wedding?"

The Divrei Chaim's illustrious son shook his head in the negative.

"I have come to give you whatever you need to make this wedding."

The *tzaddik* looked at him, a question in his eyes.

"All I can tell you," said the German Jew, "is that your father sent me word that it's time for me to pay back the money I owe him—through you. Please tell me exactly how much money you need to make this wedding the right way."

The *heilige* Rabbiner Halberstam made a calculation. A meticulous calculation.

Interestingly enough, the sum he arrived at tallied exactly, to the penny, with the amount of money that the German

Jew owed the Divrei Chaim. The businessman repaid the loan, and added a generous wedding present as well. Then he returned home, marveling the entire way at the wisdom, foresight, and sheer righteousness of the holy Divrei Chaim.

———➤•◀———

I knew many, many stories which I told and retold. They all highlighted the Divrei Chaim's greatness.

Chaim Schenker was an extremely wealthy man, one of the richest Jews in the Sanzer region of Galicia.

But it wasn't always that way. He'd started off penniless. The journey from a poor man to a rich and influential one took place over a fairly short amount of time. And it was all due to the Divrei Chaim's advice.

In those days, many Jewish people rented public houses (pubs) from the local gentry. It was a way to make money, yet it was easy to lose money as well, because of all the army and police officers who ate and drank for free, and all the poor gentiles who couldn't afford to pay for what they drank, though they frequented the inns every evening.

They were great customers. They just weren't that great at paying for what they consumed.

Chaim Schenker had been offered a deal on a tavern/ inn in the town of Oshpitzin (Oświęcim in Polish), a town which would later become notorious by its German name. He would have jumped at the opportunity to manage the tavern, were it not for the fact that Auschwitz was not known as a place with a high level of religious observance. In fact, its inhabitants were more on the modern side, and this gave Chaim pause. How could he subject his children to unknown, possibly very adverse, influences?

But a Chassid has a Rebbe, and Chaim's rebbe was the Divrei Chaim. It wasn't long before Chaim Schenker found himself in Sanz, asking his spiritual mentor how to proceed.

"Move to Oshpitzin," the Divrei Chaim instructed his Chassid, "and your move will, *b'ezras Hashem*, have a positive influence on the entire town. Once your family is living there, other Chassidic *Yidden* will join you, and the entire town will take on a more Chassidishe flavor."

Chaim needed no further encouragement. It wasn't long before he'd moved his entire family "out of town" to the spiritual wilds of Oshpitzin, where he rented the local inn/tavern from one Count Roosocki, who owned all the lands in Oshpitzin, Zasole, Brzezinka, and Babice. The fabulously wealthy count rarely graced the village with his presence. He was too busy enjoying himself in the more lively metropolises of Lemberg and Lublin.

From the start, there were problems of a financial nature for Chaim to deal with.

Foremost among these was the neighboring countries' practice of charging a very high import tax for wheat—a practice that made it almost impossible to sell the local crops in a foreign market. This kept the price of wheat low and the people impoverished, which meant that they had a hard time paying for their bit of drink.

It was difficult to earn a living from a bunch of poor peasants. But that wasn't even the main problem. No, that paled beside the drought that arrived during Chaim's very first year as the tavern's manager. Suddenly, even those peasants who'd managed to put aside a little money to spend on drink found that they could no longer manage even that. The situation looked bleak. It didn't appear as if Chaim was going to be able to pay his rent.

No drunkards were coming for their daily drink.

No money was entering Chaim's cash register.

Now what?

The situation was desperate. Chaim couldn't see any way out.

With no choice, he traveled to Sanz to ask the Divrei Chaim whether he should pack up and leave Oshpitzin.

⟶•⟵

Chaim entered the Divrei Chaim's *Beis Midrash* and asked the *gabbai* to let him in to see the holy *tzaddik*. The moment he entered the Divrei Chaim's inner sanctum, even before he managed to open his mouth, the Divrei Chaim met his beseeching gaze with his confident beautiful eyes and said as follows:

"If you can't manage to raise the rent, then you should purchase the entire estate."

These were cryptic words. Chaim couldn't afford to pay rent on one building. How on earth would he be able to afford the entire estate? What was the Divrei Chaim talking about? What miracle was he referring to?

Chaim had no idea. But his rebbe had finished and the audience was clearly at an end.

Obviously the future would show what the Divrei Chaim had in mind.

⟶•⟵

Count Roosocki, the master of the estate, was largely uninterested in the inner workings of his properties. Like many people born into wealth, he had no understanding of what it meant to work for money; consequently, he was in no position to ensure the success of his holdings. He had hired a Polish property manager years before. This manager lived in an ostentatious mansion on the estate's grounds, a house that served as the headquarters from which he lorded it over the poor peasants. The man was a cheat, a drunk, and a liar and he treated everyone who had any dealings with him in a terrible manner. But what did the count know about all this?

The answer? Nothing.

The count didn't really care. He was busy. Drinking. Going to parties. Riding horses. Gambling. He had neither the time nor the inclination to involve himself in the affairs of his estate. That's why he'd hired Pavel in the first place.

At times, however, the count recalled his father and how responsible a man he'd been, and he was ashamed. That was why he decided to pay a surprise visit to the Oshpitzin estate one day, out of the blue.

One minute, everything was normal, and the next, the count had taken the town by storm in his almost-royal carriage, a pair of majestic steeds straining as they pulled the heavy vehicle through the muddy streets. The crest of arms clearly showed who had come for a visit. By rights, the people should have been a little more enthusiastic; he was their liege after all. But, the citizens showed a marked lack of excitement, and even a tinge of animosity. He couldn't understand it.

Wherever Count Roosocki went and whomever he spoke to, he sensed a certain inexplicable aloofness—even anger.

"Why so down in the mouth?" the count finally asked a peasant he encountered.

The man mumbled something about the count's agent Pavel, and his mistreatment of everyone under his control.

"Pavel is mean to you?"

"He treats us as if we were his personal slaves. He's a terrible manager and a horrible person. Nobody likes him."

"Nobody?"

"Nobody at all. He's an evil man, a sinner, an oppressor of the poor."

The count found these accusations extremely disheartening. He wasn't a bad man, just a pleasure-seeking one. He knew himself. He wouldn't be able to return to the gaming tables and his fancy friends in Lublin while the people who lived on his lands were being treated so shamefully.

The next day found the count hard at work, poring over the estate's books. He wanted to know exactly where things stood. He planned to make some order in his "house." But the more Count Roosocki studied the books, the more discrepancies he discovered on almost every page. It took him a little more time, but he eventually reached an inescapable conclusion: Pavel was stealing from him, and had probably been doing so for years.

Roosocki sent for his estate manager at once. But Pavel had a keen nose for which direction the wind was blowing, and was long gone.

The count was very discouraged. Not only couldn't he return to his mansion in Lublin, but he now he had to remain behind to try and make everything right again. Wherever he turned, there were problems that needed fixing. The whole estate was falling apart. The houses were in disrepair, the animals hadn't been properly fed and watered, and the workers hadn't been paid. The count wanted to sell off the entire estate—to simply wash his hands of his problems, as it were. But Pavel had already sold all the crops and nobody wanted an estate without any crops to sell.

The count was at a loss.

It was at this exact time that the Austrian government began planning the future route for their Vienna-Cracow-Lemberg railway line. The count, hearing this, saw a means of salvation if he could just persuade the Austrian government to make his estates part of the future route. He submitted such a plan to the Austrians and took out a mortgage from a local bank at the same time, in order to develop the estate farms to a more productive and profitable level. The bank approved him for a much higher mortgage than he'd expected, due to the fact that it appeared the Austrian government was going to route the train through Oshpitzin.

But just as Count Roosocki's problems appeared to have come to an end, disaster struck.

The local Oshpitzin council decided that they weren't in the least bit interested in having the future railroad run through their area. The farmers were afraid that sparks from the train's wheels would shoot out at the neighboring fields and cause fires which would burn down all their property. Everyone had some complaint to make about the planned railroad. They took their issues up to the government. They made sure to send all their objections to the board that made the routing decisions, requesting that it refrain from routing the train through Oshpitzin at all.

Count Roosocki became extremely apprehensive. He was fed up with the estate and all its headaches. He didn't want to have to deal with the Oshpitzin council, the peasants or the government. All he wanted was to go home so he could play, hunt, drink his brandy and scotch, and go back to his "real life."

He thought and thought about his dilemma. Finally, he recalled Chaim Schenker, who had rented the tavern from him, and who might very possibly be interested in cranking their relationship up a notch.

So he sent for Chaim, who came expecting the worst and found an entirely different and not unpleasant reception awaiting him.

"Take a seat, my friend," the count began.

Chaim sat on the couch.

"As you no doubt know," the count went on, "I've been having trouble with my estate here in Oshpitzin. In fact, I would be more than happy to sell you all my lands. All you would need to do is take over my mortgage." The count went on talking, explaining the fine points of their business transaction, but Chaim's mind was elsewhere.

Just a few days earlier, the Divrei Chaim had told him some very prophetic words. "If you can't afford to pay rent," he'd said, "then just purchase the entire estate."

Chaim didn't ask any questions, because there were none to ask. The Divrei Chaim had told him what to do. He was going to purchase the estate.

Within days, Chaim's luck had turned around dramatically.

The Austrians paid no heed to the peasants' petition. The railroad was indeed scheduled to run through Oshpitzin. And Chaim received enough money from the government to enable him to pay up his mortgage in full.

And if that wasn't sufficient good news, His Majesty's government in England came to the conclusion that it would be a good idea to lower the taxes on imported wheat. All the surrounding European countries followed England's lead in the matter. Which meant that the price of grain once again rose and rose.

Chaim Schenker became the richest man in the entire district.

All because he followed my *elter Zeide's* advice.

CHAPTER THREE

AROUND 1863, THE FIRST TELEGRAPH OFFICE opened up in Sanz. This was a cause for great rejoicing, because it allowed what had previously been a secluded world to become somewhat accessible.

In the past, every village had lived its own life, with no way to contact any other place except by letter, which took a long time, or traveling there in person. Now, however, all one needed to do was send a telegraph, which didn't take long at all. Suddenly, communication had come to Galicia.

A telegraph, and then, many years later, a telephone.

What a miraculous achievement!

To stand in Lemberg and speak with someone in Lublin! What a miracle, what a wonder!

(Of course, the usage of the telephone would herald an unparalleled ability to indulge in *lashon hara*. The *yetzer hara* never ends the battle to cause us to sin; it merely updates its attempts and clothes them in different guises. But that is neither here nor there.)

It would be quite some time before people would have the option of using a phone whenever they wanted. At the start, the cost of using the telephone for even a very short time was prohibitive, so of course every word one said was weighed again and again. (Which, ideally, is how we all should live!)

Suddenly Sanz and the rest of Galicia had entered the modern world.

But before that era arrived, things were very different.

The following incident gives us a glimpse into how life was before the advent of the telephone and other modern devices.

———◦◦———

Duklah was a little town.

It had a *shamash*, just like every other little town. His name was Reb Tzadok Hakohen Steiner. One of his tasks was to lock the *shul* every night after the last person had left.

Reb Tzadok took his job very seriously and never neglected his responsibilities. One afternoon, Reb Tzadok's son Yaakov was playing outside the *shul* when he grew tired and decided that it was time for a nap. Without thinking too deeply into the matter, he entered his father's *shul*, lay down on a bench, and nodded off.

The boy slept and slept. He was comfortable and in no hurry to wake up. Meanwhile, Reb Tzadok finished his chores for the evening, snuffed the candles used for illumination, and locked up the *shul*. Then he left the building, unknowingly having locked his young son inside with no way to get out.

It wasn't long afterward that Yaakov awoke. You can imagine the terror he experienced when he realized where he was and that he was completely alone. The *shul* was almost morbidly dark and extremely frightening. A tiny light flickered by the holy Ark. The scene filled his young mind with dread and he became hysterical. Crying fiercely, he raced to the exit and fearfully tried the heavy door, but it was locked and bolted shut. He knew that further prodding was useless.

The door was not an option. But what about the windows?

He ran over to the windows, but they were far too high for him to reach.

Shaking and shivering, the young boy retreated to the relative safety of a nearby bench. He crawled underneath, determined to remain there for rest of the interminable night.

When the *shamash* walked into his home without Yaakov by his side, his wife was understandably concerned and inquired as to where her child was.

Reb Tzadok realized that he had no idea where Yaakov was. Extremely concerned and agitated, he began searching for his son in every place that he could think of—all to no avail. Yaakov was gone. Dark thoughts began filling Reb Tzadok's mind.

"Wait a second," he suddenly yelled. "He's probably in the *shul*!"

Reb Tzadok couldn't get back there fast enough. He raced through the empty streets, turned the key in the lock, and opened the *shul* doors as speedily as was humanly possible. The room appeared to be completely empty. The *shamash's* heart fell to his boots. Where was his son? What had happened to him?

Yaakov, still hidden under the bench, was frozen in shock and terror. Hearing the key turning in the lock, his heart was filled with thankfulness at his salvation. He wanted to emerge from his hiding place, to show his father that he was fine and unharmed, but terror had rooted him to the ground, as if his feet had sprouted tentacles which were tying him in place.

"Is he there? Is Yaakov inside?"

Reb Tzadok's wife, who had come along for the search, was becoming more and more dismayed. He wanted to give her good news, but the minimal light that his swinging lamp provided was not sufficient illumination to show them their son, still cowering beneath his bench. Consequently he remained unaware of the fact that the boy was hiding in very close proximity.

"I don't see him," the father said gently, his heart thudding like a falling stone.

"He's really not there?"

"It doesn't look like it."

They turned to leave. Yaakov, realizing that he'd better speak up if he didn't want to be locked up in the *shul* for the rest of the night, strove mightily to overcome his shock and hysteria. "I am here!" he cried. "I am here!"

So they rescued him, took him home, and fed him soup.

But the overwhelming fright he'd suffered in that hour under the bench, and the horrible fear of being locked up in the *shul* again after salvation had finally been at hand, combined to strike the young boy dumb. Yaakov could not speak. He had lost his ability to utter a word. It was a terrible tragedy.

The *shamash* was close to the town's rav. Rav Avigdor was a *tzaddik* and a special man. He was also the Divrei Chaim's brother. He listened to the painful tale quietly, and when Reb Tzadok had finished unburdening himself, told him that he would write a letter to his brother in Sanz.

"My brother is a famous miracle worker," he explained. "I hope he will be able to assist you in your hour of need as well."

And he did as he had promised.

The letter went out in the usual way.

It left Duklah by personal messenger, headed for Zmigrod. The messenger made his way over rough, unpaved roads filled with potholes that could swallow a coach whole. He arrived in Gorlitz, traveled onward to Gribow and finally, after a lengthy, exhausting journey, entered the environs of Sanz where the letter was delivered to the Divrei Chaim to read.

The Divrei Chaim responded to the sad story by informing the messenger that he would be visiting the township of Duklah soon and would deal with the sensitive matter himself. It was another four weeks before this response reached the family, who were beside themselves with worry and fear for Yaakov's future. Eleven weeks after the *shamash's* son hid under a bench in the dark *Beis Midrash* and lost his ability to speak, the Divrei Chaim of Sanz arrived in Duklah.

It wasn't long before the afflicted child was brought before him, like a patient to an esteemed world-renowned doctor. The Divrei Chaim opened up a book of *aleph-beis* and laid it on the table in front of the boy.

"Can you please read the *aleph-beis* for me?"

Silence. The boy might have been deaf and dumb. There was no indication that he had even heard the words that had been said to him.

The Divrei Chaim picked up his pipe. Clutching it in his hand, he used it to give the boy a gentle knock on the right shoulder.

Yaakov uttered not a sound.

The Divrei Chaim was undaunted. He repeated the tap on the left shoulder as well.

The onlookers looked on hopefully. Would it help? Would Yaakov start talking again?

No. He remained as quiet as a mouse.

The Divrei Chaim was unperturbed.

This time he struck the boy between the shoulder blades.

Suddenly Yaakov opened his mouth and began reciting the letters of the *aleph-beis* as if he'd never stopped talking. As if it were the most natural thing in the world for him to speak!

It was a great miracle—that much was clear.

The Pshevorsker Rebbe remembered Yaakov years later, from when he took over his father's job as *shamash* of the *shul*. He recalled an old man of seventy. An old man who spoke in slow, slurring, careful tones. Like someone who was never sure of himself when it came to opening his mouth.

The people of the town used to repeat what the holy Divrei Chaim had said at the time.

"Yaakov was lucky that he wasn't locked in the *shul* after his bar mitzvah," the *tzaddik* had commented, "because the long-departed souls that come to occupy the empty *shul* at night would have called him up to the Torah for an *aliyah,* and in that case, Yaakov would have surely died. The terror would have been too strong for his young heart."

Soon after that episode, the telegraph was installed. Life began moving at a faster pace. Sanz was coming of age, and the world was changing more rapidly than anyone knew how to deal with.

———⊷∘⊶———

The following account came from a man who merited seeing the Divrei Chaim as a young boy. He never forgot what he witnessed.

As a child (he said), my father shared his ardent love and respect for the Sanzer *Tzaddik* with all his family. Every Shabbos meal came accompanied with countless tales of the Divrei Chaim's greatness, his incredible insight into every man he met, and his lofty *neshamah* that shone forth like the morning stars. The Divrei Chaim was a *malach* (angel). He was as close to *Hashem* as a human being who lived in this day and age could become. He was a miracle worker, able to see through every person that he met.

I can't even describe to you how anxious I was to meet the Divrei Chaim—how much I longed to see his glowing visage and to hear even a few words from his pure mouth and burning soul. But the Divrei Chaim was already an old man, and I feared that I would never have the opportunity to catch a glimpse of him with my own eyes.

And then the *Seder* came along, and I heard the news. News that shook me to my very core.

News that made me want to dance in the streets, singing joyously and thanking the Creator again and again.

My father was planning a trip to Sanz right after *Pesach*. He needed to ask the Divrei Chaim's advice regarding which *yeshivah* I should attend in the near future.

I waited, my heart beating furiously. Would he voice my greatest wish? Would I be granted the chance of a lifetime?

"Of course, you will come with me," he said.

Here it was—the promise I'd been waiting to hear for so long. It was a dream come true! The year was 1872, and I was ten years old.

Do you think I slept at all till the arrival of the holiday? I can't imagine that I did. How could I have fallen asleep, when my most cherished hope was about to come true? And even if I nodded off from sheer exhaustion, my sleep was filled with dreams of saintly men with eyes that glowed like the sun and a smile that spoke of beautiful, happy moments dwelling beneath the shadow of the *Ribbono shel Olam*. I had no doubt that my father's rebbe, the Divrei Chaim, fully resembled an angel of *Hashem*. No doubt at all.

How would we get to Sanz? That was a good question.

We could have traveled by train. After all, Europe's rail system was already highly efficient by then, with train lines running through every city.

The trouble was, we couldn't afford to travel by train. Such an extensive trip was far too costly for us. That was why we took the train for only one leg of our journey, from Dembitz to Tarnow. I wished we could have taken the train the rest of the way as well, but it was not to be. On the other hand, traveling in the style we did meant that we'd receive a lot more reward from heaven, in recompense for the hardships we endured on the way to see the *tzaddik*.

How did we get there?

We hitched. Plain and simple.

One *shtetl* to the next. One town to the next. A village here, a city there. It was a never-ending journey filled with towns and roads and forests that looked exactly the same. The people, the animals, the weather—all the same. Cold and windy and miserable. And then came the downpour. That happened as we were walking from Tarnow to Sanz. An endless, bone-drenching storm. It felt as if we would drown before we even arrived in Sanz.

I closed my eyes against the storm and waited for it to end. I hoped that tomorrow would be warmer, drier, and more peaceful, and that the storm wouldn't stop us from reaching Sanz. We hid in a large barrel that had housed whiskey in its former life. Now it served us as protection against the elements, giving us something to hold onto so we wouldn't be swept away with the rain and the wind.

All in all, it was a nightmare of a journey. By the time we reached Sanz we were barely alive. My father and I were bedraggled, frozen, sneezing and wheezing, and fatigued to the bone. But the joy inside our hearts far outweighed any physical discomfort we might have felt.

Who cared about sleeping or eating, when you were about to see the Divrei Chaim?

Who cared about being warm and dry, when you were about to see the Divrei Chaim?

Who cared about the fact that you had been reduced to skin and bones, when you were about to see the Divrei Chaim?

Not me, that's for sure.

We arrived in Sanz on a Thursday afternoon. My father knew his way around the town; consequently, it didn't take us long to find somewhere inexpensive to stay.

Was it a nice place with decent furnishings?

Probably not, but who cared about that? Not us.

We settled in and unpacked our meager belongings, filled to the brim with the joy of our arrival.

And then our mood was shattered into a million pieces.

Our host informed us that the Divrei Chaim, holy spiritual leader of thousands, had just returned from the cemetery.

Why had he been visiting the cemetery? Was today the *yahrtzeit* of some long-gone *tzaddik* that we'd forgotten about?

No. The reason the Divrei Chaim had been visiting the cemetery was because his daughter had just passed away. He was now in mourning.

The Divrei Chaim was a mourner. He'd be sitting *shivah* in his home. My father didn't know what to do. His disappointment was intense. He'd been yearning to see his rebbe, had dragged himself through half the mud of Galicia for that purpose, and now his rebbe would doubtless be unavailable to him at least until the *shivah* was over.

I was very bitter and disappointed, too.

"You know we won't be able to remain here until the end of the *shivah*," father told me sadly.

I nodded. Of course I knew. Father had barely been able to afford this trip. But to stay in Sanz for another week? That was pushing the boundaries beyond the possible.

The thought of leaving Sanz without at least catching a glimpse of the Divrei Chaim made me want to cry out in pain. It was a physical ache. We had traveled so far, suffered so much, deprived ourselves of food and sleep, and nearly drowned in a violent storm—and now we wouldn't even be able to see him? We could not allow that to happen!

My father, being well known in the city, received special permission to join the Rebbe's *minyan* that evening for *Maariv*. We entered the Divrei Chaim's *Beis Midrash*. My father took a seat at one of the tables, opened a *sefer*, greeted an old friend. I, on the other hand, had but one thought on my mind: to catch a glimpse of the holy man. I looked around the room, trying to discern if the Rav was already there or not. Then I noticed a door at one side of the room that was slightly ajar.

Was that the door to the Divrei Chaim's private study?

There was only one way to find out.

I approached the door and peeked through the crack, about as excited as a child is capable of being. My breath came in gasps. My hands were clammy to the touch.

Suddenly a whirlwind entered the room. He had arrived through a different door. I turned around in time to see a slight man of relatively advanced age and short physical stature who walked with a limp. Yet this man was not only walking, he was almost running! He was here, he was there, looking at this one, moving past that one, his entire body one fluid field of motion. The Divrei Chaim had just returned from the cemetery. Just come back from the land of the dead. Just finished burying his daughter.

There was water in the room, and he washed his hands. Then he said the *berachah* of *Asher Yatzar*. I have never heard anyone recite the *Asher Yatzar* with such utter *d'veikus*, such complete adoration and devotion to *Hashem*.

I couldn't move. I couldn't do anything. I was rooted to the spot, rendered speechless at the sight of such intense *Avodas Hashem*. I had just seen a *malach*!

That was how he was. He never stopped moving. It didn't matter if he was sitting or standing, alone or with a group of Chassidim. He was always moving. There was electricity everywhere. It was amazing—almost otherworldly.

We were in the middle of counting *Sefirah*. If you know anything about Chassidim, I don't have to explain how seriously they take the concept and *mitzvah* of counting the *Omer*. They scream and dance and cry and shut out the world, reaching for the loftiest heights, striving to move worlds and become better people—all during one ordinary *Maariv* prayer.

I have seen many people counting the *Omer* with fervor and holiness. But their *avodah* was nothing, nothing, compared to the Divrei Chaim and his spiritual conquest of the empty earth and its meaningless pursuits. He was on a whole different plane when he counted the *Omer*. The happiness, the sheer, unbridled excitement and the absolute wonderment that he exuded all came together in a fashion that I would never, ever forget for the rest of my natural life, and probably in the World to Come as well.

This was the Divrei Chaim's philosophy: "A *Yid* is a soldier on the battlefield of *Hashem*. And, like a true soldier, he will not desert the battlefield in times of war, even if he's injured, even if he's bleeding, even if he has no chance of turning the tide. So long as he's still able to move, a *Yid* must act. To serve *Hashem* with complete joy, even when it's difficult, even when it seems as if we are losing the battle. We must devote our lives, our selves, our very souls, to serving *Hashem*, and we must do it as long as we're alive. Even if we're bleeding, even when we're hurt. Serving *Hashem* must come first. Always and forever."

Needless to say, I never forgot that visit to Sanz, or my brief glimpse of the Rebbe and the uniqueness that never ceased to inspire those around him and to command their respect and reverence.

———≫·•·≪———

I hope you're beginning to get an understanding of my ancestry. The Divrei Chaim was my great-grandfather, Zeide Shaya'le's Tatte, and I thought about him a lot, as did my father and the rest of our family. As, above all, did "*der Zeide.*" The Divrei Chaim had been so holy, so special, such an inspiration to *Klal Yisrael*. I was a Halberstam and I was so proud to share such an exalted lineage.

That was why these stories that I'm telling you are not just stories. They are my history. They are what makes our family what it is. If you want to understand me, you need to know and understand these tales. Because they are our past.

———≫·•·≪———

In the village of Sanz, people did not go to court. If you had a problem with someone, you summoned that individual to *Beis Din*. Everyone respected the *dayanim* and obeyed their decisions, so there really was no need to have recourse to the secular court system at all.

That was why everyone was so surprised when a certain Yossel Zeltzer refused to comply with a summons to the local *Beis Din*.

The case had been brought by someone named Perlstein, who had a monetary claim against Yossel. When the messenger arrived with the summons, Zeltzer brazenly insisted that he would most certainly not grace the *Beis Din* with his presence, and that if Kalman Perlstein wanted to have it out with him, it would only be in a secular court of law. This stubborn declaration came as a huge surprise to the entire village. Not because Zeltzer was being stubborn; Zeltzer was known as a stubborn man. No, the surprise was that he was insisting on a secular court of law. This was very strange. If anyone in Sanz contemplated doing such a thing, that person knew that he would be shunned by all. Why was Zeltzer going in this direction? Nobody had an explanation for this most unusual phenomenon.

Now, if it ever happened that a person refused to accept the ruling of the highest *Beis Din* in Sanz, he had another alternative. That was to submit his case before the Divrei Chaim himself. The *Gadol* would deliver his decision, after which there would be no further questions. All would submit to the Divrei Chaim's *psak*. But the first step was to appear in front of the *Beis Din*. Yossel Zeltzer was completely out of line.

What made it even stranger was the fact that Yossel wasn't a bad man. He was a respected personage in Sanz, a *Yid* who knew how to learn, a *Yid* with a seat on the *Mizrach vant*, a *Yid* who had been content to blend in with the rest of his peers. What on earth was going through his mind?

The *Beis Din* received Zeltzer's response and was most displeased with the sheer insolence and arrogance displayed by the little man.

Immediately, a stronger summons was dispatched to Yossel, who reacted with the same inexplicable disdain and detachment.

"If Kalman wants to have it out with me, it will have to be in a court of law, not the *Beis Din!*"

Sanz buzzed over this bizarre turn of events like a hive of crazed bees, while Yossel kept to himself and evidenced zero concern regarding the rest of the town. The Kreiser Rav sat on the *Beis Din,* and Zeltzer's refusal to show himself was the ultimate act of chutzpah. One simply did not behave this way to the son of the Divrei Chaim.

The messenger made his way through the streets of Sanz once again. In his hands, he held a smoking bomb: the *Beis*

Din's ultimatum. Either Yossel Zeltzer agreed to submit himself to the Sanzer *dayanim* and to obey their *psak*, or the *Beis Din* would be forced to place him in *cheirem*. Being in *cheirim* meant a swift social death for a person and his family. Nobody would talk to him or his wife and children, nobody would do business with him, nobody would even pray with him in *shul*. He would be a non-entity in Sanz. And the question remained: Why? Why was he doing this? Why was he willing to destroy his life for no obvious reason? It made no sense.

Clearly, the matter had gotten out of hand. Yossel would come to his senses—he *had* to. His entire life was at stake! What could possess an individual to bring himself to complete ruin like this?

The messenger presented Yossel with the ultimatum. Yossel perused the short missive, his face turning a lovely shade of purple. His response: "If the *Beis Din* dares to place Yossel Zeltzer in *cheirem*, then Yossel Zeltzer will be forced to put them in prison!"

News of Yossel's audacity spread through Sanz like wildfire. The city was absolutely enraged. Words could not express the disappointment and fury they felt toward Zeltzer and the dybbuk that had apparently taken hold of him. His behavior was unforgivable. Whatever happened now, Yossel had just stepped beyond the pale of Jewish life. He was done for.

Nobody knows whether the *Beis Din* actually carried out the *cheirem*. There was no elaborate ceremony to banish him from the community. Nothing like that occurred in the public eye. Perhaps the *Beis Din* did it quietly.

There is no dispute, however, about what happened two days later. It is documented and was personally witnessed by many. The populace of Sanz arrived in the main *shul* for *Shacharis* (morning prayers), to discover the following words scrawled across the wall in the boldest, blackest lettering possible.

"Yossel Zeltzer, *Yimach shemo,* **is in** *cheirem."*

After that, there was no turning back. It was the proverbial straw that broke the camel's back.

It was not long before Yossel filed an official complaint with the police against the *Beis Din* of Sanz. His main issue was with Rav Aharele, the Kreiser Rav, the Divrei Chaim's son.

The Kreiser Rav was a modest man who loved peace. Very much like his namesake, Aharon *Hakohen*, he would go out of his way to make sure that everyone got along and that disputes and controversy were kept away from Sanz. But he was not a tough personality, and Zeltzer took true advantage of that. In fact, Zeltzer went so far as to name the Kreiser Rav as the main reason all of this had occurred. In the file that he submitted to the secular court of Sanz, he claimed that the entire scenario was Rav Aharele's fault, and that he must be put in jail to be taught a lesson.

The city was up in arms, with some wanting to simply cart him away one night and throw him off a bridge or some such thing. On the other hand, that wouldn't have solved anything, because the matter had gone far beyond that point. The gentiles were now involved and things were out of control.

Unbelievable as it may seem, Yossel did not stop going to *shul*. It didn't matter to him that nobody was willing to sit beside him, or that everyone looked at him with a gaze that spewed venom. He reacted with indifference. But the people of Sanz had had enough of this incredible audacity and they would tolerate it no longer. Suddenly, fights began to break out between the citizens of Sanz and Yossel and his children. Wherever they found themselves, tensions would start to rise and shouting and physical altercations would commence. Soon enough, Yossel had to turn to the Polish police for protection. And even that was not enough to convince the people to leave him alone. They hated him with all their hearts and wanted to throw him out of their town, head first.

Zeltzer's next brilliant idea was to sue the *Beis Din*. This would have made sense, except that nobody in Sanz was willing to testify against the *dayanim*. So Yossel brought in the gentile judges, to witness the way the youngsters of Sanz were making his life a misery. Naturally, the elders of Sanz begged the teenagers not to attack Yossel or his family in front of the judges, but try talking sense to a teenager. Of course, they didn't listen.

The situation grew worse and worse, and unfortunately, much of the well-deserved abuse directed toward Zeltzer took place where the gentiles could witness what was happening. One particular incident aroused the ire of the judges who witnessed it, in large part because the towels and prayer shawls that were being hurled at Zeltzer hit one of the judges himself.

This turned an already inflamed situation into a raging bonfire.

<hr />

The day of the court case arrived. A bitter day for all of Sanz.

It was a traumatic time for a community completely unused to seeing its members rebelling against the accepted *gedolim*.

It was almost as if *Tishah B'Av* had come to Sanz:
Groups of Chassidim assembled in every *Beis Midrash* to recite heartfelt, fervent *Tehillim*, begging *Hashem* to save their rabbis and judges from the misplaced anger of a man gone insane. What was going to happen now? Would the secular court move to convict the Jewish judges? Would

the *dayanim* be sent away to jail? Would Zeltzer succeed in wreaking even more havoc?

Everyone looked to my Zeide, the Divrei Chaim, for reassurance. But his attitude was unfathomable to the average *Yid* in Sanz. He didn't seem perturbed in the least. Life in his home went on as usual.

Nobody knew what to make of this strange situation. The Kreiser Rav, the Divrei Chaim's beloved son, might very well go to jail, yet his distinguished father remained seemingly uninvolved.

On the day of the trial, the Kreiser Rebbetzin couldn't control herself any longer. In a state of great agitation, she entered her father-in-law's study, where she begged him for salvation in a choked voice and with fresh tears running down her cheeks.

"Please *daven* for your son," she implored.

The Rav arose from his seat. His answer was quick and to the point. And it was not what the Kreiser Rebbetzin wanted to hear.

"One may not! One may not!" the Divrei Chaim cried out, piercing distress evident in his voice. "*Kol mai d'avid Rachmana, l'tav avid.* Whatever *Hashem* does is for the best!"

"But it will be a *chillul Hashem* if the Kreiser Rav goes to jail," the Rebbetzin gasped, her heart pounding with fear and stress.

"A *chillul Hashem,*" the Divrei Chaim repeated wonderingly. "A *chillul Hashem* is when a *Yid* forgets the *Ribbono shel Olam* for even one moment. *That's* a *chillul Hashem!*"

The family came to the belated realization that the Divrei Chaim refused to approach the authorities on his son's behalf. But they were desperate. Zero hour had arrived. It was almost too late. If only the Divrei Chaim would consent to speak with the Polish authorities, things might still be sorted out. They decided to approach the Belzer Rebbe and ask him to persuade the Divrei Chaim to speak to the proper individuals. Everybody respected the Divrei Chaim. If he would speak up, the Poles would listen. Could the Belzer Rebbe change his mind?

The Belzer Rebbe tried his best. He did, in fact, request that the Divrei Chaim intercede with the authorities on behalf of his son and the other *dayanim* of the *Beis Din*. The Divrei Chaim's response to the Belzer Rebbe's request was to go into a deep bout of meditation. When he finally emerged from his reverie, he related the following tale to the assembled.

—————

"The Maharam of Rottenberg was abducted by the gentiles and incarcerated in prison while his captors negotiated with the Jewish community for his redemption. The price went far beyond the realm of the reasonable, but the community was willing to go that extra step and raise the money to free the tremendous Torah scholar. The average citizens could never have managed to raise the necessary funds, but the wealthy members of the community stepped up, willing to be *moser nefesh* for their Rav.

"But they had not taken the Maharam himself into consideration.

"When the holy *tzaddik* heard the astronomical sum of money the non-Jews were demanding for his release, he barred the community from redeeming him.

"'If you pay the price they want, it will convince the gentiles to do the same thing to someone else—and demand even more money next time. I will not allow you to redeem me. It's against the Torah.'

"The Maharam was true to his word, and he remained in prison for the remainder of his natural life. Though his body was imprisoned in an earthly jail, he still managed to teach Torah to a group of spiritually uplifted students who grew under his expert tutelage even in the depths of their medieval captivity. He chose to serve *Hashem* in a prison cell rather than cause his brethren additional harm."

You can imagine how the assembled felt upon hearing the Divrei Chaim's words. He'd just dashed any hopes they might still have cherished for keeping the Kreiser Rav out of jail. The Divrei Chaim was clearly not prepared to intercede on his son's behalf. It didn't seem as if there was anything left in the world to be done for R' Aharele.

Would he and the entire *Beis Din* go to prison?

It was up to the gentiles. Terrible thought.

In the end, the *dayanim* of Sanz did go to prison for six weeks.

Each week felt like an eternity. Every minute was an hour — a day — a year. It was pure *Gehinnom* for those holy *Yidden*. Even worse; it was precisely during those six weeks that the bulwark of Polish Jewry passed away. The Divrei Chaim was *niftar*, taken from this world right in the middle of his *Beis Din's* terrible ordeal. The authorities were as sympathetic as they knew how to be. They allowed the Kreiser Rav out of prison so he could attend his father's funeral.

They allowed him out escorted by heavily armed guards, as if the pious rabbi was going to attempt an escape.

The moment the funeral was over, R' Aharele was spirited right back to jail. There would be no sitting *shivah* together with the rest of the family. He was a criminal, after all. When their sentence came to an end, the *dayanim* were released and allowed to return home, weakened and saddened by their agonizing ordeal.

And what about Yossel Zeltzer, that once-respected member of the community who'd sat on the prestigious eastern wall in *shul*? What happened to him?

Well, for one thing, his children strayed completely

off the path of righteousness and ceased living a life that retained even a modicum of religious observance.

And Yossel?

It was not long before he lost his entire fortune. Absolute, irrevocable, financial ruination. What was worse, not a single member of the Jewish community would look him in the face for the rest of his life. He was completely shunned. Forever. No one would *daven* with him, do business with him, eat a meal with him, or even exchange a few words with him.

——————

There were many other stories. I have an almost endless supply of tales about my ancestors. I begged to hear them, was put to bed with them, and repeated them to anyone who would listen. But it's been so many years. Most of them are long gone.

CHAPTER FOUR

EVERYBODY KNOWS ABOUT THE BAIS YAAKOV movement, and how it began in Cracow under the leadership of a "simple" seamstress named Sarah Schenirer. Books have been written about the single-mindedness of this unassuming woman who changed the world. But there's a little more to the story than most people know.

There was a whole group of women in Cracow who were friendly with Sarah Schenirer and who felt very strongly that a Bais Yaakov-type movement was what was needed to save the religious girls of Poland from assimilation. My aunt, Reb Shlomo Bobover's sister, was part of this group, as was my mother. My mother never told me about this. She never related that she'd had anything to do with Bais Yaakov and its inception. It was Reb Shlomo Bobover's sister who shared this hidden part of her past with me.

"Your mother had recently been married," she told me. "She looked around and saw which way the wind was blowing all over the country."

My aunt went on to describe my mother's observations. Who were the educators in every Jewish home in Poland?

The women.

The women were the first step when it came to disseminating proper *hashkafah*. They were the ones who instilled the infants with Torah values. It was the mothers who chose the first words their children would hear and the type of atmosphere in which they would be raised.

"Your mother looked around her, and she was afraid," my aunt told me. "Those were not good times. The Haskalah, Zionist, and Communist movements were grabbing hold of thousands of young minds and not letting go. And the impressionable young girls weren't receiving enough in the way of *chinuch*. It was no wonder that they were drifting away. Despite the fact that their daughters were no longer on the same page as their parents or brothers, families continued marrying them off to Chassidishe boys, as if they hadn't changed at all.

"It wasn't long before the effect of these differences was felt, and couples began streaming to the Polish *Batei Din* requesting a divorce. It was becoming an epidemic. Your mother was a smart woman. She wanted to understand why this was happening – to get to the root of the matter. She began to investigate, and it wasn't long before she had a clear and decisive picture as to the cause of all the discontent. It stemmed from the teachers.

"The girls were going to teachers to learn how to read in Hebrew and Yiddish. Many of these teachers were affiliated with the Haskalah movement. They didn't always try to influence their students in an overt manner. But when a person studies with someone who has corrupt values, it seeps into her mind and manner through daily conversation. If at first the changes were subtle, by the time the girls were finished learning from these 'enlightened' teachers, they had been completely brainwashed and corrupted from the Torah life they'd grown up with. They wanted something different. They wanted to experience the world.

"Your mother felt that the girls should be taught, just like the boys. Maybe not Gemara, perhaps, but certainly *Chumash* with its commentaries, *Navi* and *Halachah*. They didn't have to become Talmudic scholars, but there is a huge gap between being a scholar and not even being taught the basics.

"What to do? Your mother thought and thought, and eventually she came up with an idea. Around this time, she'd had her first child, and the doctors told her that it was possible she would never have another. The double emptiness in her soul, stemming both from the fact that she seemed destined to live in a quiet, almost empty home, along with the terrible situation of Poland's Jewish girls, caused her to come to a decision along with a friend of hers – a young woman named Sarah Schenirer, who was childless and also searching for a way to change their world.

"The idea of Bais Yaakov had to become a reality. Your mother and Sarah Schenirer were two glowing lights in a void of endless darkness.

"While the vast majority of the women in their social circle were the daughters and daughter-in-laws of rabbinical figures and couldn't even suggest such a radical concept, Sarah Schenirer had no such problem. She didn't come from a rabbinical home and nobody would look askance at her if she began an educational movement. Your Zeide Shaya'le gave his full support to their project and its goals, even granting them the usage of the *Ezras Nashim* as a teaching facility. He was devastated by the recent spate of Jewish divorces all over Poland, and agreed with your mother and her devoted friend that the only way to save the girls of *Klal Yisrael* was by teaching them Torah and showing them the beauty and knowledge that belonged to them as well as to their brothers and fathers.

"Sarah Schenirer and your mother were overjoyed to save the Jewish girls of Poland. They had a burning desire to do so, and filled their days and nights with whatever was needed to carry out their mission. They were willing to devote their lives to the cause and didn't care if there was opposition. Bais Yaakov began with a handful of young women, future teachers, who were completely dedicated to the idea of saving the girls of prewar Europe, one mind at a time.

"Your mother remained an active part of the first Bais Yaakov until her family — flaunting every prediction the doctors had made, and making medical history — began to grow, and she was forced to spend more time at home."

———————

In the beginning, the fledgling movement didn't even have a name.

They asked my mother, "What should we call the group?"

My mother wasn't sure.

"Why don't you ask your husband?"

My father, who thought a school for religious Jewish girls was a wonderful idea, pondered the matter and came up with a name that would endure for generations to come.

"Call it Bais Yaakov, the house of Jacob," he suggested. "A house where the mothers of *Klal Yisrael* will learn to educate their children."

And Bais Yaakov it became.

POLAND
THE WAR

CHAPTER FIVE

MY PARENTS DECIDED TO MOVE TO CRACOW A short time before our entire world caved in. The gigantic war that would change the face of Europe was almost upon us, but we were still living in our own happy bubble, clueless about the fast-approaching turmoil.

We moved to Cracow when my oldest brother, Chaim, became engaged to Mariam Brucha Halberstam, a cousin of ours and the daughter of the Kalishitzer Rebbe from Reisha. The plan was for the young couple to marry just before the High Holy Days, after which my brother would succeed my father as Rav in Sucha. My father, in turn, was going to take over Zeide Shaya'le's position in Cracow. *Der Zeide* was very old by now, and my father found himself spending increasingly more time by his side.

Life in Cracow of 1939 was the equivalent of being stuck on a boat speeding toward a whirlpool that threatened to suck us all into its undertow, but without our realizing that anything was wrong.

Sure, some people listened to the radio and heard that powerful *meshugene* from Berlin ranting and raving as he spewed his hateful philosophy. Sure, he'd penned his magnum opus titled *Mein Kampf* while in jail, where he outlined his plans for the Jews of Europe.

But Berlin was so far away. How serious could the situation be? After all, everything around us seemed exactly the same.

But the days passed and more and more Jewish refugees arrived from Germany, finding shelter in several school buildings near the Zeide's house. They had nothing. No food. No clothing. Of course, my parents and *der Zeide* did what they could for the German Jews. And we children were sent shuttling back and forth with steaming trays and pots of delicious Shabbos food for those who had so much less than we did. There was an *eruv* in Cracow, and the arrival of Shabbos meant that we children entered delivery mode.

The German refugees were grateful beyond belief.

Not long before, they had been living in their own beautiful homes and apartments. For many of them there had been plenty of money, and they were the proprietors of businesses that had been in their families for generations. Now, they had nothing. But they were overjoyed just to be far away from the Nazi monsters.

We were so happy to help them. We only prayed that the evil that had forced them to leave their homes would remain where it all began.

Unfortunately, that was not to be.

I was very young. How was I supposed to know that the greatest war of the century had broken out? The Nazis had managed to grab the Sudetenland by dint of Hitler's superlative negotiating skills. Europe's very real fear of being drawn into the same kind of conflict that had decimated millions of its youth just a few short years before was starting to come true. The Nazi soldiers were warmly welcomed into Austria, where the populace treated them like long-lost sons returning home. The Germans called their entry into Austria "the flower war," because that's what their conquerors were showered with: flowers. Austrian children were Hitler's youth; Hitler was a native son, after all. They were actually proud that they'd spawned such a monster.

After that, the West backed down. Chamberlain returned home waving a paper that was worth less than nothing. The Allies were a bunch of dithering old women scared of their own shadows. The United States, under Roosevelt, had no interest in fighting another European war. It didn't seem as if there was any real leader who could take control of the situation. Hitler was sitting in the driver's seat and seemed poised to remain there for the foreseeable future.

And then German foreign minister, Joachim Von Ribbentrop, and Russia's Vyacheslav Mikhailovich Molotov met in Moscow and signed a treaty that would ensure that the German Wehrmacht would remain untroubled as it stormed Poland in a Blitzkrieg—a lightning-quick war, overpowering and destroying the entire Polish army in a just over a month's time. This was no surprise, considering that the Poles were using horses against what were at that time, the most modern war machines invented by man. No, the surprise came from a different direction altogether.

How had Russia and Germany, long-time enemies, come to make peace?

How does something like that happen?

If *Hashem* wants it to happen, it happens. That's the answer.

And then the Nazis came. It was the first day of

September 1939. And nothing was ever the same again.

———————

If I close my eyes for a second, I remember the marching. The sound of those marching feet was the most hated, most horrible sound a person can imagine. It was the sound of a terrible machine of hate moving relentlessly closer and closer. It was a feeling of constriction, as if they were choking us without laying a finger on us.

We'd had no idea that this nightmare machine was approaching. One second, life was still peaceful.

And the next?

Next came the bone-jarring sound of thousands of jackboots marching toward us, intent on our destruction. Their evil eyes were a collective, unsullied blue as they marched, bayonets at the ready. They were the face of Germany, the evil from Germania that the Talmud had written about, and we were the innocent Jewish children of Poland.

And then, in one instant, we were innocent no longer.

The Nazis arrived. The marching chilled our blood. And we knew: every dream had come to an end.

Suddenly, Zeide Shaya'le was not in Cracow any longer. He was taken to Lemberg, along with his wife. Tatte did not go with him. He was busy categorizing and caring for *Der Zeide's* extensive library, *sefarim* that *Der Zeide* had written, *sefarim* written by Reb Shaya'le's father, the Divrei Chaim, and *sefarim* written by Reb Shaya'le's father-in-law, Rabbi Yaakov Tzvi Rabinowitz of Porisov.

Meanwhile, our days took on the quality of the worst curses from the Torah. We were sitting at home — waiting — waiting for the sound of those cursed, infernal boots on the stairs. Were they going to come today? In a minute? In an hour?

We might have been little children, but all you had to do

was look at those strutting men in their long gray army over-coats, metal helmets, and rifles, and you knew. You knew in the pit of your stomach, in your very essence, that these were the worst kind of people alive, that their entire being was dedicated to evil.

Who would they take? Who would they grab? Would your brothers and sisters still be sitting at your side in ten minutes?

If I close my eyes for a second and think back, I can still hear those boots — like millions of evil machines marching of their own accord. Relentless killers, every one of them.

They turned all of Poland into one giant slaughtering ground, where instead of killing animals for food, they murdered human beings to satisfy their crazed ambition to rid the world of the Jewish people.

They conquered Poland in just over thirty days. What good are horses in the face of tanks? No good at all. The German planes swooped down from the sky, bombing the stuffing out of Warsaw, and reducing that fair city to a mound of rubble, as every civilized country in the world looked on in terror. Thousands perished in the bombings, lying on the cobblestones with no one to pay them their final respects, because everyone was too busy trying to save his own life to spare a thought for the dead sprawled in the streets.

It was very late at night when Mama woke me to say goodbye to Tatte. I had been sleeping, and when she woke me up it felt as if I was in the middle of a dream — in the middle of a nightmare, because Tatte wasn't the father I had always known. This Tatte standing before me had no beard! I couldn't even be sure that he was really my father. My father had always had a beard. I looked at Mama in wonder. How did she know that this was Tatte? It didn't look like him!

No beard.

No *peyos*.

His face was bathed in tears. I looked at my mother, as though searching for confirmation that it was really him.

"Tatteshe," I sobbed. His beard was gone! Nothing was the same. It was the beginning of the end.

He said goodbye to me, and gave me a *berachah*. I still couldn't believe that this was my father. I cry now, just remembering the scene. The grandson of the Divrei Chaim, without a beard! What had the world come to?

Tatte ran away that night with my brother Chaim and my cousin. They all fled to Lemberg.

Dogs and cats were freer then we were. They weren't afraid of humans, while we had to be fearful all the time. The Nazis began pulling people off the streets. We girls were terrified of them, but our fear was nothing compared to what the men and boys felt. They could be pulled off the street at any time, with no warning.

A beard became the most dangerous thing in the world. You have no idea what tremendous *mesirus nefesh* it took for a Jewish man to keep even the slightest sign of Jewishness on his person. A few wispy hairs on a sixteen-year old face could drive a German officer to heights of insanity. He might pull out every hair, ignoring the victim's screams of agony, or he might just shoot the Jewish boy dead. You could pretend that you had a toothache by wrapping a cloth around your jaw, and it might even work. Then again, it might not. And if it didn't, you might not live to the end of the day.

People who would never have dreamed of touching a hair on their faces were forced to shave. Because if you kept your beard and the Nazis caught you, it meant indescribable torture. Laughing like crazy people, they would pull and tug at your essence, yank at your Jewishness, rip out the holy clumps of hair by the roots as though trying to suck the very *Yiddishkeit* from your countenance.

Every boy over fifteen had to shave, although some refused and didn't care what happened to them.

But many shaved. Who could blame them?

The pain! Forget the humiliation. We were beyond that. The pain was so bad that the humiliation meant nothing. I remember how they caught a man in the inner courtyard of Zeide's building. How he screamed as they tortured him. How we would lie awake for hours at night hearing the screams float up toward us from the street, as the prowling denizens of the netherworld found yet another victim to torture and punish for the crime of being a Jew.

And always, with laughter.

Sometimes, even today, it takes me hours to fall asleep because I float backward in time. Back to Cracow. I lie in bed and I can still hear the shouts of the men who were caught, and the inhuman laughter of the Nazis as they hurt them so badly.

I knew who and what those Germans were from the first instant I laid eyes on them. I knew it in the very marrow of my bones.

And they will get exactly what's coming to them. There is no scorekeeper like *Hashem*.

My mother's sister moved in with us in Cracow. She arrived from Tchebin with most of her children. I think the Nazis had already taken away her husband. Soon afterward, we received the letter in the mail. A letter from the Germans.

"You must report to such and such place by no later than. . . for resettlement."

They wanted all the Jews where it would be easy for

them to gather everyone together and move us to the camps. Many followed their orders and reported where and when they were told. My mother was different. She decided that she would never follow the Nazis' orders. We were not going to go anywhere voluntarily. Meanwhile, we lived from hand to mouth. It was here that Mama's "*shterntichel*" was a real lifesaver. Every Rebbetzin owned one.

They were magnificent objects.

Shterntichels were kerchiefs encrusted with pearls, gold, and other precious materials. They were worn on Shabbos and special occasions and, in our previous life, had turned Mama into a queen every Friday night.

I can visualize Mama sitting at the end of the dining-room table, graciously presiding over her family like a regal matriarch, her smile lighting up the room. The *shterntichel* shining and basking in the glow of the Shabbos candles and their ethereal light.

Now the *shterntichel* had a new purpose: providing us with life and sustenance. Every so often, Mama would cut off a few of the pearls from her beautiful kerchief to sell, and the money would support us.

The loftier the queen, the more practical she can be.

My mother, the sheltered Rebbetzin, also had the foresight and the rare acumen to open a business. She went into the bread business. Retail, of course. There were bakeries still operating in Cracow. Some of them were prepared to sell us bread. Some of them were even willing to deliver bread to us, which we would then resell to others who weren't able to go get the bread themselves.

Sometimes, however, I had to pick up the bread. That's when it got tricky, because if you were caught carrying a loaf of bread, you could be shot. It was that easy to die. You had to be very careful.

I slipped through the shadows. I learned how to move

in a world of soldiers, as if I was living on a battlefield. I learned how to tread lightly, huddled close to the sides of the buildings. Sometimes I almost ran into the dreaded soldiers. Sometimes they emerged from an alleyway on patrol just as I was coming the other way, and almost stumbled over me. I would be forced to run for my life into a nearby courtyard, breathing hard from the exertion, certain that they had seen me and would come running after me. They would take away the bread and send me away, somewhere very bad where nobody ever smiled.

But I managed to elude them every time. I learned how they walked and could hear them from far away. I could almost smell them as they approached. My senses were finely attuned to danger. I had become a tunnel person, a smuggler, someone who knew how to operate like a chameleon, and I delivered the loaves of bread to people who couldn't get around to buy their own. And the people paid. Because people have to eat.

⇒•⇐

There was a boy.

Just a boy.

He was hiding from the enemy. Running for his life.

When the knocks came, it sounded as if an army was banging down our door.

I ran to answer. The boy stood in the doorway. His eyes bulged with fear and beads of sweat were plastered to his forehead. He looked as if the Angel of Death was literally right behind him.

"Please let me in," he begged. "The Nazis are right behind me. They want to kill me!"

He looked at us, the ultimate question in his eyes. Would we care enough about a fellow Jew to try and save him, or would we be too afraid for ourselves?

"Come in, come in, quickly!" Mama ushered him into our apartment. From afar, we could hear the shouts of the soldiers as they yelled and banged on apartment doors. The tread of their heavy boots made our hearts beat rapidly in terror. We stuffed the stranger into a tiny closet with a well-hidden entrance, hoping against hope that the soldiers would miss it, that the boy would escape.

And then we waited for the enemy to come.

As I waited, I pictured the young boy stuffed into that tiny closet, his face shoved against the wall, his hands clammy, and his young heart terrified. I felt so terribly sorry for him. He was just a little older than I was. *He's just a boy. Hashem! Save him! Save him!*

The Germans arrived. They banged on our door. We held out as long as we could, but we had to open up eventually. They would've broken down the door otherwise.

They found the boy.

They were better than us. Like highly developed predators, they sniffed him out. They smelled the blood and headed for the hiding place like cats after a mouse.

They ignored us. There was almost a feeling of, "We can't be bothered with you now. But we'll get you tomorrow."

They were two young men. Hair the color of yellow straw. Light blue eyes. Sweet Aryan youth. They went through that house like a whirlwind, ripping up carpets, knocking over bookcases until the *sefarim* went flying from their places and flopped to the floor with cracked bindings and squeals of protest.

They knew every trick in the book. They knew where to bang to check for hollowness, they knew what floors to smack, where to knock, what was really a closet and which a decoy. And when they found him, as they'd known they would, they pulled him out of that closet and went to work on that poor boy with a vigor that smacked of sick enjoyment and twisted minds. They beat him as if they were being paid for every blow. In the middle of the dining room. In front of us. Before the eyes of little children. The boy's screams were like nothing I'd never heard before in my life.

Those screams still fill my mind today.

———✦———

And so began our years of exile.

It was still early in the war. The Nazis hadn't put a wall around us yet, or ordered us to wear the yellow stars that singled us out for death. We were still able to move relatively freely. The curtain of utter darkness had yet to descend.

Jewish Cracow was divided into two parts. Jews were ordered to depart from the larger section where there was no ghetto, and move en masse into the smaller part: the ghetto. It was small enough to ensure that the Germans wouldn't have a hard time controlling their prisoners. The Nazis were still in organizational mode, still unsure how they were going to bring their grandiose plans to fruition.

You have to understand: killing millions of people is no easy undertaking. It took the efficient Germans quite some time to figure out exactly how to carry it out. Eventually, after much thought and trial and error, they developed the correct formula. But that came after they tried using gas chamber trucks (where they would stuff as many people as possible into the back of a truck and kill them using poison gas) and *Einsatzgruppen*, select groups of German soldiers who traveled through Eastern Europe, going from town to town and murdering the Jewish inhabitants in cold blood.

They tried many different ways. But it was slow going.

As I said, killing millions of people is not easy.

Eventually, they devised the perfect system. In every town, city, or village the Jews were moved into a single neighborhood, so that they were concentrated into a smaller area than they'd inhabited previously. These moves made it easier for the Germans to round up the Jews when the time came, and transport them to destinations like Bergen-Belsen, Auschwitz, and Treblinka.

So it was in Cracow. The Jews of that great city were ordered to leave their homes and herded into one section of the city. Since Cracow was so large, it was difficult for the Germans to enforce their orders. That was why we were able to ignore them for a while and pretend that we would get away with it. But deep inside, we knew that you can't outsmart the devil.

One afternoon there was a knock on the door. We ran to open it up. A seventeen-year-old girl was standing on our doorstep. A lovely young girl with thick, lustrous black hair and shining eyes.

Chaim's *kallah* (betrothed).

We ushered her into the apartment with great excitement, so happy to spend some time with the girl that was going to become our "sister." After my mother had served her the best of what we had, it was time for our *kallah* to tell us why she'd come.

Her eyes were focused demurely on the floor and Mama understood that she was here on a matter of some sensitivity. We left the room.

"Why have you come, *zeeskeit* (sweetheart)?"

Mariam Brucha, Chaim's beautiful *kallah*, was crying. The tears cascaded down her wan young cheeks.

"What is it? What's wrong?"

"I need *der Mama's* permission."

"Permission for what?"

It was hard for her to get the words out.

"Tell me, sweetheart," Mama said soothingly.

"I need *der Mama's* permission to sell my ring."

She'd finally gotten the words out. Slowly Mama drew the story out of her, helping her with words when she ran out of her own. Her family had no more money. Selling the ring would allow them to survive. Could Mama find it in heart to forgive her for even contemplating such a thing?

Mama ordered her to sell the ring.

What was a ring compared to the life of a daughter-in-law?

I think that was the last time we saw Chaim's *kallah*. She would eventually join the partisans and fight in the European forests for as long as she was able.

She did not survive.

I never forgot her or her smile, her vitality and vivacious personality. I loved her, and I lost her. One more of many.

———◆———

For the time being, we stayed where we were. We huddled in our homes, afraid of our shadows, terrified to leave the four walls that provided us with the illusion of safety, while the Germans did their best to hunt down every last one of us. They sent letters to the Jewish population, ordering them to their new destination inside the ghetto walls. And people actually listened to them! But not us. We weren't prepared to listen.

Eventually, though, we were forced to leave.

Mama did not want us to move into the ghetto. Ghettos were bad places. Mama knew this instinctively. If we were being forced into a place where the Germans wanted us, it was not for our benefit. Consequently, it was time to move on.

And so, we left Zeide's Cracow house for the village of Bochnia.

The trains of Europe would take us there. The trains were still our friends then, though later they would become our enemy. We were supposed to wear an armband as a sign that we were Jews, but we wore nothing. We were not inclined to obey their orders. We didn't travel in one group. That was too dangerous. Taking a page from Yaakov Avinu's book, we split up. At least, this way, someone would survive.

A non-Jewish friend of my mother's accompanied us. I think she was a doctor's wife, and in Poland that meant a lot. She knew how to carry herself with the grace of the upper class, an innate, intangible ability that the average Polish non-Jew recognized and by which he was cowed. We boarded the train two at a time, and she sat nearby. And we were comforted by her presence, despite the fact that, were we to be caught, her presence would not have helped us at all. We would not have called out to her, and there would not have been anything that she could have done to save us.

But at least someone would have known.

And someone would have been able to tell our mother with authority that they'd taken us away. At least that. Because there's something important in just knowing. Not knowing is a terrible form of hell.

We traveled by ourselves, just two little girls. The farther we were from home, the lonelier we felt. The beautiful Polish countryside flashed by, freeze-frames of cows and barns and people who were lucky enough not to know fear and who didn't even know that their lives were so richly blessed.

All too soon, the wheels began slowing down as we approached the station at Bochnia. We had arrived.

———◦———

My oldest sister, Devora, had been given an assignment by my father: to oversee the hiding of the family's *sefarim*. I was only a little child, so I don't have a clue as to how, exactly, she was supposed to accomplish this monumental task. Suffice it to say, she did not travel with the rest of us. She was left behind in Cracow and had to get to Bochnia on her own. And while the rest of us made it there without incident, Devora was not as lucky.

The train left Cracow, with Devora aboard. Outwardly calm, inwardly trembling. There were soldiers all over the place.

"Papers!"

A soldier was standing in front of her. She didn't have the necessary documents. In short order, Devora was arrested and escorted off the train.

None of us had any idea that she'd been caught by the enemy.

A short aside while we're on the topic of Zeide's *sefarim*. About twenty-five years ago, in the late 1980's, several of us returned to Poland for a specific purpose. My older sister Devora had been given a mission by my father, to save as many of Zeide's *sefarim* as possible. Saving the family was vital, but saving Zeide's *sefarim* came a very close second. And it wasn't only Zeide's *sefarim*. There were precious manuscripts from Zeide's father, the Divrei Chaim of Sanz, as well, the lifeblood of thousands of Jews who had revered him before the war.

The delegation included Devora, her husband, a cousin whose father was also a prominent Rav in prewar Poland, and me. A group of dreamers. My cousin was hoping to find her father's *sefarim* as well. Unfortunately, it turned out to be an extremely frustrating trip. Though we searched everywhere we could think of, we found nothing. Zeide's *sefarim* were gone. It was as if we were losing everything all over again. We'd had such hope that we would return home with something tangible from our holy ancestor, but it was not to be.

Everything had vanished.

From Cracow we journeyed on to Warsaw, where the Polish Museum of Pre-War Jewish Culture is located. The museum was a veritable treasure trove of books, documents, and family heirlooms carrying the most illustrious names of Jewish Poland on their covers and etched in their tarnished silver.

My cousin was lucky and unlucky at the same time. We discovered several of her father's *sefarim* in the museum. That was the lucky part.

Unfortunately, the authorities would not let us take anything home.

No amount of protestations helped. They didn't care who we were and that these books were rightfully hers. Poland was still under Russian authority back then, and the Communists were adamant. The *sefarim* remained right where they were.

My cousin was shattered. She'd been filled with such hope that she'd be able to return home with a piece of the past, and now her hopes had been dashed to the ground.

Decades have passed since that terribly disappointing trip. Decades when it seemed as though *Der Zeide's sefarim* were gone forever. It was only very recently that I heard how some of them were found many years ago. How numerous *sefarim* were discovered after the war and taken away, never to be seen again. How some were even sold for huge sums of money!

But these were our family's *sefarim*. They should have been returned to us. By rights they belonged to my uncle, Zeide's sole remaining son.

And though we had no money then, we would have taken loans to pay for them. We would have done whatever we needed to do, to return Zeide's *sefarim* to his family, so that his legacy could be passed on from father to son.

We still want our *sefarim* back. More than anything else. Our money was taken away; but money comes and money goes. Zeide Shaya'le's *sefarim* were our lifeblood. We feel the loss and pray for them to be returned to us one day.

———•◦•———

Except for Devora, we were all back together again, crowded into a tiny apartment in Bochnia. We were supposed to live at the Rav of Bochnia's house, but the Germans had gotten to him first. He was no longer among the living. So we were forced to move in somewhere else, mourning our holy cousin even as we tried to find our feet in a new home, a new environment, a new life on the run.

Soon enough, we realized that something was wrong. Devora should have been here by now. She was a very responsible girl. If she had not yet arrived, it was a sure sign that something had happened to her.

The only thing that could have happened was an arrest. She must have been caught up in the German net. Nothing else would have stopped her from joining her family. But how were we to uncover the truth? We had no idea when or where she'd been arrested. On the train? In the city?

What to do?

It was then that Mama turned to the Landau family.

Both Osher and Leizer Landau were men who loved to learn, and they also had numerous business connections—especially Leizer Landau, who'd owned a herring business in Poland which he eventually transplanted to Israel after the war. Even the Germans purchased goods from them. Reb Osher Landau lived in Bregal, not far from Bochnia. If there was anyone who could find out what had happened to Devora, it was the Landau family.

Within the next few days, someone came to visit us with the information. Maybe they were sent by the Landaus, or maybe not. We didn't know. We were informed that Devora had been arrested by the Germans and was currently residing in a jail in Tarnow.

At that point, Mama was no longer in Bochnia. She'd gone to Bregal to see Osher Landau, hoping to glean information about Devora. Time was of the essence. Mama had to be informed of the latest developments so she could decide on a course of action. My older sister Rivka and I were chosen to make the journey to Bregal, find my mother, and tell her what we had learned.

We were happy to make the trip (anything to help get Devora back!) but it would turn out to be a journey straight out of hell. Try to imagine the scenario: two little girls, setting out by foot from Bochnia to Bregal. It was winter. Freezing cold. Rain, sleet, sometimes snow. The ground was a morass of mud and we had no boots. There was a road between the two cities, but we dared not approach it because it was constantly in use by the German military. Our unwillingness to be seen by the Germans didn't leave us much choice; we had to stay off the road.

We could see the road from the fields through which we trudged, hugging the Polish haystacks, trying our hardest to avoid cows and sheep and Polish farmers. We were on a mission and we were determined to carry it out, come what may. Never mind the icy rain that struck our frozen faces, or the mud that caught our feet and tried to swallow us alive.

We were going to save Devora, and we would do whatever it took.

The ironic thing about all of this was the fact that, while we were marching along to Bregal, Mama was boarding a wagon to take her back to Bochnia. She had met people in the know who'd filled her in on everything that was happening. She'd already received the information that Devora was in Tarnow and was now on her way to us! We were risking our lives for nothing.

(I later found out that Reb Osher Landau was murdered by the Germans. By the very German, in fact, who used to do business with him. The *hakaras hatov* (gratitude) of a Nazi.)

My sister and I walked for hours. We finally arrived in Bregal as day was rapidly shifting into a bitterly cold night. Not knowing where else to go, we made our way to a relative's home—a prominent Rebbetzin. She welcomed us warmly. Somewhat to our bemusement, we learned that Mama was no longer there. She had gone back home while we were trudging through the cold and rain to fetch her.

Morning dawned. We'd had a harrowing trip the previous day and were very tired. The Rebbetzin let us sleep late, gave us breakfast, and arranged a ride for us back to Bochnia with someone who graciously agreed to allow us to travel hidden under a pile of straw in the back of his wagon. We made our way to the departure point, climbed aboard the wagon, and were promptly covered with bundles and bundles of itchy, scratchy straw. We huddled together under the straw, trying to stay as warm as possible. But it was an intensely cold day and we were soon shivering profusely.

And then it started to rain.

Our tears merged with the rain. Rivka's teeth were chattering as the wagon rattled along. "I'm so cold, Sima," she whispered. Her lips were blue, her eyes feverish.

"Me, too."

"I can't go on like this much longer."

"We're almost there. We'll be home soon."

"I know, but I feel like I'm going to die soon if I don't get out of this rain."

What was I to answer to that? Exhort her to be brave and strong? She *was* being brave and strong. All I could do was reassure her that our suffering, our terrible ordeal, would soon be over.

But soon wasn't soon enough.

A torrential rainstorm hit us with tremendous force. The straw that had been sheltering us couldn't hold up against that cloudburst. Within minutes, it felt as though we were in a swimming pool—a mucky, repugnant swimming pool filled with floating straw that did little to keep the downpour away from us. Two little girls, clinging to each other at the bottom of a wagon rapidly filling with a soaking deluge mingled with straw.

This was where my beloved sister Rivka got sick.

It was a sickness that attacked her bones. She became crippled after that trip. All because of one wagon ride under the straw.

And the world asks us why we insist on remembering what happened in Poland!

———————

We finally arrived back in Bochnia. Mama was home.

"Mama, Mama," I called out, anxious to share the news of Devora's incarceration. "Devora's in the Tarnow jail!"

A look of infinite sorrow and fatigue crossed her delicate features. Mama saw how we had suffered, and she cried with us. Rivka was put to bed to recover from the trip. (Not that it would help.)

It's an interesting thing. Some of the events we experienced in the war appeared logical to us and were easy to comprehend. Yet there were others for which we had no explanation. Devora's release from the Tarnow prison fit right into the latter category.

To this day, nobody knows why the Germans released her without a word of explanation. Why did they permit her to leave their prison unharmed when they were killing Jews all over Europe? Why would they allow a young Jewish girl to walk off with a chance at life?

The best reason I can come up with is that the Germans were not yet focused on the women and children at this point. They were still busy rounding up the Jewish men. They didn't mind letting her out, because they knew that sooner or later they would find her again, together with the rest of her family. And then — they would finish the job.

But Devora cheated them.

She survived the war.

CHAPTER SIX

THE YEARS FROM 1941 TO 1943 WERE A TIME of constant upheaval and movement. Of shuttling back and forth between the open ghettos of Bochnia and Bregal. Sometimes we had a place to live in Bochnia and sometimes we had one in Bregal. But nothing ever lasted, and there was always a reason why we needed to run from one to the other.

Rivka and I had made it back to Bochnia, though she'd almost died en route. Devora had been inexplicably released from prison in Tarnow. We would have liked nothing more than to be allowed to live quietly in Bochnia. But we had nowhere to stay. Nobody had enough room for us. Nobody could muster up the energy to care about so many other people, when they had their own families to worry about and feed and clothe.

So we had to leave Bochnia.

Mama, however, did not despair. That concept wasn't part of her mindset or her vocabulary. Never mind that she'd always been well taken care of, first as the daughter of a prominent family and later as the wife of a rav. She was on the run now, and she adapted to her present situation with alacrity.

"It's time to go back to Bregal."

"Do we have to walk?"

"No, this time I've arranged for someone to drive you with a horse and wagon."

This sounded much more appealing than walking through the rain and cold for hours. We traveled back to Bregal, extremely grateful for the comparatively easy trip. The clip-clop of the horses' hooves merged with the flick of the reins and the coughing of the driver to create another childhood memory. Soon enough, we were back in Bregal with our caring relative, the Rebbetzin. She lived alone in an apartment that was big enough for all of us. This was a place where we would be able to settle down, at least for a while.

It was as if two worlds coexisted, side by side. On one side was our world of the wandering Jewish refugee on the rickety wagon and, on the other, the monster Panzer tanks of the Wehrmacht that crushed everything in their path. Elderly Jews bowed down by packages shuffled along the side of the road as German military vehicles zipped past, sending clouds of Polish dust into their suffering faces. Two separate worlds, thrown together by the whims of war.

It took some time, but eventually all eight of us were back together with Mama at the home of the Rebbetzin.

In Bregal, Mama revived her bakery business, but this time with cookies instead of bread. You might ask how it was possible to even consider selling cookies at a time when bread was so scarce! The answer lies in the fact that the loaves of bread were large and bulky. It was easy to get caught smuggling such bread. Cookies, on the other hand, were small. They were easy to transport. And we kept the price down. We charged a minimal fee for those delicious cookies.

Consequently, Mama's bakery business flourished.

Bread would have been preferable. But if you can't have bread, people with make do with anything. Even cookies.

———※○※———

It would have been nice if we could have remained in Bregal for a while. We would have liked to find some peace and tranquility after the sheer insanity of the last few months. Rivka needed to recuperate from her illness: the wracking cough that wouldn't disappear, the gaunt, emaciated frame that was becoming thinner and thinner despite Mama's frantic attempts to heal her. Now that the sickness had taken hold, it wasn't prepared to relinquish its grip. The truth was, Rivka was dying, plain and simple.

But we couldn't remain in Bregal for one simple reason.

Space was not an issue. We had the Rebbetzin's apartment. For once we had all the space we could possibly use.

It was the typhus.

My friends, how fortunate we are to live in a day and age where cleanliness and sanitary measures are given such respect and high priority. You cannot even imagine what Bregal looked like when that typhus epidemic broke out. It was as if an enemy had attacked us without a war! There was absolutely nothing to do against this relentless yet invisible force.

Bregal was a typical Polish town. The majority of the homes did not have running water. But typhus was racing through the town like a fire through dried leaves, and the sick needed water.

"Water, water, water!" You could hear the screams emanating from every window and doorway.

There was a pump in the center of the town. Bregal's water source.

People would bring the dying to the pump. Sick people on the cusp of death, shaking and shivering as the Angel of Death hovered over them in the city square. Have you any idea what it is for a child to see other children lying helpless on the cobblestones, knowing all too well that they have only hours to live, crying to their mothers for water, begging them to make the pain go away, while their mothers and fathers can only look on helplessly, with no tools to combat this vicious tyrant, no medicine to give their suffering children?

Why didn't they leave the patients in the privacy of their own homes? Didn't they deserve that much?

But the families of the ill couldn't leave their loved ones to die in "peace" in their beds, because the Bregal houses were small. Leaving a dying typhus patient in a house full of children would ensure that the entire family caught the dreaded disease. I, who had grown up in a sheltered environment, who had never witnessed violence or anguish, was now seeing and hearing children screaming for relief—and there was nothing anyone could do for them. Those pitiful cries! And the pain! Typhus is incredibly painful. How they suffered! Some of them begged *Hashem* to take them so the pain would stop.

Imagine what they were thinking. *I'm dying, and nobody can do anything for me.*

It's ironic. While the epidemic was running its course, the Nazis were nowhere to be seen. Sully their perfectly polished shoes with the dirt of suffering humanity? Place themselves in possible contact with a zone of contagion? Not on your life! Bregal was safer than ever—yet at the same time more dangerous than ever before.

The epidemic lasted for months.

Months of torture.

Months of the most horrible sights the world had to offer.

It wasn't long before Mama decided that we were moving back to Bochnia, and the sooner the better.

It was a miracle that we escaped with our lives.

———————

Bochnia was such a tiny place. Just a few streets, that was all. And yet, in those few streets you could find greatness.

The greatness came in many forms. Some were people who had already been looked up to before the war broke out. Leaders, rabbis, prominent personalities. And there were others. Simple people who did great things.

As in every town, the Germans utilized the Jews to do their dirty work for them, pitting Jew against Jew in a way that took a terrible situation and made it unbearable. But that, of course, was the enemy's intention.

Every town had a council of Jews, the Judenrat, who acted as the conduit to carry out the Germans' bidding. It was these Jews who informed the rest of us of the German orders. They announced when the Jews had to work, and where. Frequently, these men shouldered the most terrible burdens, because it was they who knew when the next "*razzia*" (police raid) was going to take place. Sometimes they warned their fellow Jews; many times, they didn't.

Yet who can judge anyone who lived through those times?

I certainly can't.

Bochnia had a Judenrat as well. It was their job to inform the populace that the Germans wanted them to work, that they would be expected to contribute their share to the war effort by toiling long hours in the neighboring factories. All Bochnia would hear the roar of the loudspeakers as another order was issued, and everyone would emerge from their homes to hear what the Germans wanted this time. What new misfortune had befallen them now? Nobody dreamed of remaining indoors or ignoring the loudspeakers. Everyone needed to know what was being demanded of them. Otherwise, how could they attempt to disobey?

Devora was part of a group that was sent to the towering forests nearby to cut down trees. It was backbreaking labor. She'd return home, crushed after doing work that a powerful man would have found impossible.

I was still a child. But being a child in those years did not afford you special dispensation. Especially when you had a sister like Rivka. Because of her age, Rivka had been ordered to work. But one look at her, and you knew that she was simply incapable of doing anything. That drive under the straw had destroyed something within her.

I was young enough to avoid working, but I would do anything for my sister. I would have jumped through fiery hoops if it meant that she would survive. If Rivka needed me to take over for her at work, then that's exactly what I was going to do. So I painted wooden dogs for the Germans at a big factory. I remember painting those cute little Dalmatians. It was painstaking labor. Tongue between my lips, I focused on my paintbrush, making sure that every dog had the requisite number of black spots. I learned other vital skills as well. One day we were painting toys, and the next we were being taught how to braid women's belts. We were quick learners.

We had to be.

Meanwhile, my beloved Rivka lay at home and grew steadily weaker.

To be a child in Bochnia was to live on the edge of a razor-sharp knife. The Germans had no use for anyone who couldn't produce, and of what possible use were the children of the ghetto? With the best will in the world, what was a child capable of doing?

The head of Bochnia's Judenrat had a sister who'd given birth to twins not long before. You'd think that the safest place for a mother of little babies was the home of the man who carried out the Germans' orders—the head of the Judenrat. The sister thought her babies were safe there. Consequently, she was taken unawares when a few Germans surprised her brother with a visit.

They'd come to deliver a message, but were pleasantly surprised when they discovered some Jews who needed getting rid of at the same time. Two for the price of one. Within minutes, the nine-month-old twins had been murdered, their heads smashed, despite their uncle's protests.

The Nazis finished their business and left his home. It was business as usual. Smash a few heads, bury a few people alive, shoot a couple of random passersby.

All in a day's work.

———————

The world was blanketed in a pristine carpet of white. It melted between your fingers, slipped away like the remnants of a dream. It was the darkest, bleakest time of year, a time when it seemed as if the sun would never shine wholeheartedly again.

And yet, maybe it was not so bad after all. Because even the Germans were reluctant to leave their barracks for no reason. Maybe the cold, while slowly killing us with its grasping tentacles, was protecting us as well.

It was the winter of 1942. A freezing, rainy, snowy winter replete with miracles. That was when Tatte and Zeide Shaya'le returned to Bochnia from Lemberg.

Lemberg had been an ideal place for them during 1941.

It was a huge city and there was safety in anonymity. But all that ended when it became clear that the Nazis would be taking control of the city within a matter of days. Every Jew in Lemberg was suddenly faced with a few hard choices.

To remain where they were. (Nobody thought that was a very good idea.)

To run away to Siberia. Out of the clutches of the Germans and into the claws of the Russian bear. (This meant trading the evil we knew for an evil that might be better but could be even worse.)

Or to leave Lemberg and join the rest of their family in Bochnia. The Germans were in Bochnia as well, and the ghetto was growing smaller all the time, due to constant German operations to weed out more and more Jews—but at least the entire family would be together.

Tatte, Zeide, and my brothers chose to return to us.

[Author's note: The Jews of Lemberg were treated with a brutality that was out of all proportion even when measured against typical Nazi behavior. Herded into mass graves, they were buried alive, the sounds of their screams echoing from under the churning soil as they died *al Kiddush Hashem. Hashem yikom damam*: May *Hashem* avenge their blood.]

And so, the Halberstam family unexpectedly found itself all together again in Bochnia, now residing on Balatska Street in a charming, one-family house with many rooms. It was wonderful to be living under the same roof again after so much time apart. It was particularly special to be able to spend time with Zeide Shaya'le. He was sweetness personified, and every minute in his presence was a blessing to be savored.

The love we felt for our elderly *zeide* cannot be described.

It was love in its purest sense. Love of virtue, of *tzidkus*, of sheer goodness.

———◆———

Nothing lasts forever. Here, as well, the "good" days were over almost before we were able to blink. Suddenly, the Germans didn't want children anymore. Not even for working purposes. Not even to scrub the floors of their barracks or to paint small black dots on toy Dalmatians. We were redundant, and it was open hunting season.

But we were not to be disposed of so easily. We were ghetto children. Resourceful. We did what we needed to do.

There were bunkers everywhere in the Bochnia ghetto. Every child found the bunker that was most suitable for him or her. Of course, you kept the directions to a few additional bunkers hidden in the back of your mind, just in case you couldn't make it to yours in time. The raw brain power of the Jewish people was at work here, and the people stepped up to the task with ingenuity. In one of the homes, a bunker was constructed under a staircase leading down to the basement. One of the steps slipped out easily and a child was able to slip inside. That was a simple bunker. There were other, more original, ideas as well.

The haystack bunker, for example. I don't know who created that one, because we found it ready for use, but I wouldn't have been surprised to discover that whoever it was (if he survived) probably went on to win major architectural prizes. The haystack bunker was located inside a haystack in one of the nearby fields. The haystack wasn't completely hollowed out; that would have been too obvious. Only one section could actually be opened. If you knew where to look (a big "if," because the entrance was extremely well designed), you lifted the outer wall and crawled inside the haystack. Then you slid down a pole which led deep under ground.

The sheer brilliance of the design was mind boggling. I will never understand how someone managed to build such an incredible contraption without anyone finding out. But it was done in perfect invisibility, almost as if Heaven itself had sent the children of Bochnia a bunker that was perfect for them. Adults might have been able to get inside with difficulty, but for the youngsters it was like a game. Jump inside, slide down the pole. Just like a fireman.

A bit of fun in the midst of ghetto life.

At the first sign of German soldiers heading toward the ghetto, we ran.

Of course, we couldn't head straight for the bunker. If anyone was watching us, that would have given everything away. We would have been caught and the bunker destroyed. Instead, we ran, zigzagging in every direction, sprinting into fields, doubling back, hiding behind trees — until we finally made it into the bunker.

And there we stayed until someone came and gave us the all clear.

But even if we managed to escape the Nazi net, they never left empty-handed. Someone was always caught. At the end of the day, when the all clear sounded, families were always left crying.

I was the kind of child who was constantly on the run. In my mind the Germans were the devil, and I had to escape their net. The words "trust" and "German" could never be said together in the same sentence. At the slightest sign of trouble, I was out the door and heading for the relative safety of the bunkers. On one occasion, rumor had it that the Nazis were going to really crack down. That rumor was cause enough for me to leave Bochnia altogether and escape to Bregal until things calmed down sufficiently for me to return.

The only question was how to get to Bregal. Traveling was extremely dangerous without the necessary papers, and I didn't even possess poor imitations. But precisely because we had no choice, we learned to think out of the box. There was a man who transported goods for the Germans from town to town. He owned a station-wagon type of car and the back was always filled with cartons and cans and materials that the Germans desperately needed.

He hid me under the boxes.

It was a little hard to breathe down there, but I was willing to endure any amount of hardship if it meant I would survive.

Before I climbed into the car that would help me escape Bochnia's tightening net, I bade Mama a tear-filled goodbye. I didn't ask her if I should escape. I merely informed her that I was going. You have to understand: nobody knew what to do back then. How could my mother have advised me? She wasn't a prophet! She didn't know whether it was better for me to run away or to remain.

The only thing she could do was direct me to a place where I could stay once I arrived in Bregal. And she gave me her blessing.

I was about to set out for the car, when two of my younger brothers, Shea and Baruch, came running over to my mother.

"Mama, Mama," they cried. "We want to run away, too! Tell Sima to take us, Mama. Please. We're afraid to stay behind. Mama, please! Tell her!"

My mother looked her children in the eye and in a quiet voice, most unlike her usually assured manner of speaking, she said to them, "*Kinderlach*, it's not my place anymore to tell Sima what to do, or who to take along with her when she runs. If she is willing to take you along, then you have my blessing to go. But it's up to her. The *Malach Hamaves* has been granted special dispensation in the world, and nobody knows where it's best to be anymore. If she agrees to take you, then you can go—and may *Hashem* be with you."

She delivered this short speech with moistness in her eyes and a catch in her throat.

How hard it must have been for her to come to terms with the fact that Mama simply did not know best anymore!

My brothers turned pleading eyes on me, and I acquiesced. Of course I would take them. Running away with two little boys would make things much more difficult for me. But they were my brothers. I loved them. My love was stronger than my fear.

We said one last goodbye. And then we left.

The road to Bochnia was full of Germans, as usual. Once again I found myself lying beneath packages and cartons of canned goods. I could feel my heart beating so loudly that I was sure the entire world could hear the sound of my fear. My brothers lay quietly as well. Nobody made a sound. During the war, even babies understood that they had to be quiet. Our trip was blessed with success. We were not stopped by German patrols, and nobody demanded to search the back of the car. We arrived in Bregal very late at night, utterly exhausted, our bones aching and complaining from the way we'd been forced to lie under the boxes.

We were no sooner settled in than Baruch began vomiting continuously. He went from being completely healthy to dangerously ill in a dizzyingly short period of time.

If it had been any other place in the world, I would have probably have just chalked his sickness up to a twenty- four-hour bug.

But this was Bregal. In this place, typhus was king! I looked at Shea, and he looked at me. We both knew what the other was thinking.

Had Baruch contracted typhus in the short time we'd been in Bregal? He was throwing up uncontrollably. Our hosts didn't know that anything was amiss, since we were staying on the third floor of their home and I had covered my brother with a mountain of straw to camouflage, or at least muffle, the sound of his horrible retching. It was very painful to watch his suffering. Every time he vomited, we had to move him farther into the attic and away from the straw that he'd soiled.

The situation was desperate.

I motioned Shea over to the side for a private council of war.

"Shea," I said, "I hope with all my heart that Baruch doesn't have typhus. But if he does, then he won't be able to eat the ghetto bread. It will simply kill him."

"Then we'll just have to find him some white bread," Shea replied, in the no-nonsense way that meant he was in problem-solving mode.

Shea and I left the house without a word to our hosts. The regular dark bread that people were eating wreaked havoc on a sick person's digestive system. Baruch needed white bread if he was to survive! Typhus attacked a person's stomach early on, and the ghetto bread was half raw. There was no way we could allow him so much as to taste a bite of it. As I've said, we were nothing if not resourceful—and in the ghetto anything could be had—for a price.

We returned triumphant, having obtained a well-baked roll. This was a genuine treasure. Our return to the house was once again carried out without a sound. We could never let our hosts know that they were harboring a possible typhus victim. They would have thrown us out before we could count to three. And who could blame them?

A white-bread roll. White flour. Or almost-white flour. And well baked. A delicacy beyond compare. This was what would save our Baruch.

———

Plenty of people get depressed these days.

We didn't get depressed. Not us, the children of the Polish ghettos. We were too busy fighting for our existence. Nobody knew when they arose in the morning whether this would be their final day on earth. Children looked at their parents, and a terrible fear gnawed at their insides: *When are the Germans going to take them away?*

Parents studied their children, committing every detail of their faces to memory, knowing that every moment could be their last together.

Me? I ran. That was how I dealt with the life I led. Constant running.

The Germans were coming?

I ran.

The ghetto was being searched?

I ran.

It was as if I was attempting to outrun the Angel of Death himself. We were on a ship with no captain and no dry land in sight. You could be traveling in circles for all you knew. But what option was there, other than running for your life?

———

Shea and I fed Baruch the white roll, bit by precious bit. Amazingly, he began to recover right before our eyes—leading us to the wonderful conclusion that his sickness had been caused by extreme hunger. Within a day he was back to his normal, cheerful self, and the terrible anxiety we had felt was already receding into the past. It didn't do to dwell on our close calls in the ghetto; there were too many of them. The moment a problem was taken care of, we moved on.

Three days later, we received word that the immediate threat in Bochnia had ended. The Nazis had come, rounded up whomever they could find, and left. It was time to return "home." The same driver who'd taken us to Bregal came for us, hid us under all his bundles, supplies, and boxes of tools, and drove us back to Bochnia.

And so we returned, having averted what could have been a major tragedy for our family.

CHAPTER SEVEN

I REMEMBER HOW *SUCCOS* USED TO BE CELEBRAT-
ed before the madness started. But all my memories of
those early days are filtered through a fog of elusive
threads that unravel the more I pull at them. *Succos* in the
ghetto is something else. That, I remember.

Z'man simchaseinu had arrived in Bochnia. Not much
rejoicing was taking place amidst the starved and fear-
ridden inhabitants of the ghetto. This was a far cry from
the endless singing in our festive *succah* back in Sucha, with
young yeshivah students and guests seated around our table
as the *succos* decorations swung in the stiff nighttime breeze
and Tatte spoke with wonder and awe of the *Ushpizin*. Nor
was it like Zeide Shaya'le's *succah* in Cracow, where the
Chassidim came to visit their mentor, have a piece of cake,
drink a *"l'chaim"* and listen to a deep Chassidic discourse or
a story about the Divrei Chaim. *Succos* in Bochnia was as far
away from those things as it could be.

The *succah* was tiny. But worse than its size was the fact

that we were too frightened to spend much time there. A *succah* is supposed to protect those who shelter within its walls, but even as we crept inside to eat some food and to make a *berachah*, we still couldn't bring ourselves to sing.

I think it was the night of *Simchas Torah* that the drunken German soldiers entered our home.

They didn't say much. They merely stumbled inside, looked around, went from room to room and finally began to take their leave—with Tatte and Zeide Shaya'le in tow.

It was more than the mind could absorb. One minute we were in our house, a few men dancing with the Torah, trying their feeble best to bring some rays of light and happiness into our depressing lives and, the next, intoxicated Nazi soldiers were leading my father and grandfather away.

Zeide barely lifted his feet when he walked. In fact, it was more of a shuffle then a walk. One of the Germans decided to offer a push to help the old Jew along. Rivka had never gotten over our time under the sodden straw, but she was standing. Barely. In tremendous agony, but still on her feet.

Rivka saw the German shove *Der Zeide*.

"Do not push Zeide Shaya'le!" she burst out. There was something terrible in her voice, a menacing note that those soldiers hadn't heard in a very long time. Imagine—a Jewish girl had dared to tell them what to do! The sheer temerity!

One of them grabbed her and threw her across the room, slamming her into the wall! I can still feel the tremors, as pieces of plaster rained down from the ceiling and Rivka's bruised figure slid to the floor amid a sea of physical pain such as I cannot even describe.

We thought that was the end. They would take Tatte and Zeide Shaya'le away, and we would never see them again.

Instead, a block away, the Nazis let them go.

I think the soldiers were afraid to take them in because they were drunk and could have gotten in trouble for being under the influence. Who knows? Maybe it just wasn't their time yet.

———◆———

Zeide Shaya'le was an old man. He was weary and could barely move. But his mind was sharp as a whip. He knew what was going on. People hid things from him, but it didn't matter because Zeide was *"meivin davar mitoch davar"*—he understood one thing from the next. One word here, another word there, and Zeide had put together the entire picture. That's the way he was.

Back in Cracow before the war, there had been two *gabbaim* who attended to Zeide's needs: Reb Tovia and Reb Chaim. They were extremely devoted men whose entire lives were dedicated to making sure that my Zeide was comfortable, that he had what he needed, and that his *Beis Midrash* and household functioned smoothly. Unfortunately, Reb Chaim and his wife were two of the first casualties of the war in Cracow.

Zeide had not been informed that his beloved Reb Chaim was gone. Nobody told him. People were afraid to share such news with a man of his advanced age. They were afraid for his life. But one day, Reb Chaim's children appeared in Bochnia.

Their destination?

Zeide's house. Where else were they to go?

Their father had been wholly dedicated to Zeide Shaya'le. Of course they went to his house.

The moment Zeide saw them, he knew. Nobody had to tell him that Reb Chaim was gone. He slammed his hand down on the table (I still remember that crack, like a gunshot) and screamed out, *"Oy, Reb Chaim is shoin nisht du!"* Reb Chaim is no longer here with us!"

How did he know? In his mind, there was no doubt at all. If the devoted Reb Chaim's children had arrived without their father, there was no question in Zeide's mind where their father was. He knew. He always knew.

———◆———

Bochnia was slowly being annihilated, day by day. Every time the Nazis came for a "visit," they left with a large percentage of the ghetto's remaining children. The Jewish population was rapidly shrinking.

The consequence of a Nazi roundup?

Less people residing in the ghetto.

And less people residing in the ghetto meant that the ghetto was made smaller, shrunken to fewer streets, which in turn meant less places to hide when the enemy arrived with bloodlust in their eyes.

The men had been taken first. Able-bodied workers were needed to provide labor for the Third Reich. Almost no men remained in the ghetto. It was like a ghost town. Now it was much easier for the enemy to grab whomever was left.

The fact that the ghetto was smaller, however, meant that the house we'd been living in was no longer situated within the ghetto limits. We were given a deadline for leaving the house and resettling elsewhere. And when the Nazis issued a deadline, waiting even a minute past that time was fatal.

Der Zeide was with us, and since he walked extremely slowly we made sure to leave ourselves enough time to get out of our old house and into our new place inside the newly drawn boundaries of the ghetto. We were already walking away from the house, when Zeide Shaya'le recalled that he had left one of his precious *sefarim* behind on the table.

I ran back to get Zeide's *sefer*.

I raced into the house as fast as my young legs could carry me, picked up the *sefer*, and ran back out again. *Sefer* in hand, I headed at full speed toward the new ghetto, hoping to make it there before any Nazis caught sight of me. But just as I entered the part of the ghetto where I was legally allowed to be, the *Lagerfuhrer*—the commandant in overall charge of the Bochnia ghetto—and some of his soldiers entered the street, their eyes searching in every direction for a stray Jew to kill.

"Look!" The *Lagerfuhrer* pointed me out to his men. "It's a little rabbit. A little rabbit running down the street. Isn't that cute?"

He was a tall man, and a sturdy one. From his demeanor it was obvious that he was a fellow who cared about his appearance. His hand moved down toward the gun in his holster.

I could hear the others laughing at his wit. The master race was laughing. It was a fine joke. What a sense of humor they possessed! A little rabbit running for its life.

The commandant removed his gun from its holster. Everything took on a slow-motion quality.

I was running. Over the sound of my pounding feet I could hear him slide a bullet into the gun.

And then, suddenly, he was shooting.

Bullets whistled past my head. I zigzagged along the ghetto street, past the wooden homes that sheltered the ghetto's inhabitants, past frightened eyes that peered helplessly from behind every curtain.

I darted back and forth, trying to avoid the shots. So many shots! They whizzed past my face on every side. The hunter shooting his prey.

I was running, running for my life, dust rising from the earth, the *sefer* clutched in my hand, the heart pounding in my chest, gasping for every breath, thinking that every moment was my last. And from behind, the sound of crazed laughter, going on and on like a nightmare that simply refuses to end.

And then I had an idea.

Houses lined the narrow ghetto streets. Some of them had entrances on two different streets. My subconscious ordered me to run as fast as I could into one of the houses, fly through it, and exit on the other side. Then the soldiers would be gone. The terrible, insane laughter would cease.

That's what I did.

The daughter of *Chazzan* Yossele Rosenblatt lived nearby. She had a little girl my age. I knew them well. The gate to her house was loose and I was able to squeeze through. Within seconds, I had passed through their property and was running into the door of my own house, the thunderous gunfire and evil laughter still echoing in my mind. And then I was home, telling my mother how I had just been hunted by the commandant.

Mama became extremely agitated. Instead of being overjoyed that her daughter had managed to escape being shot, she became terribly agitated.

"What's the matter? Aren't you happy that I'm O.K.?"

"Of course I'm happy! But don't you understand what might happen now?"

I thought for a moment, and suddenly I knew exactly what she meant. It hit me so hard, I felt as if I was going to faint!

The insane commandant was on the loose.

His prey had eluded him, and he was doubtless feeling extremely frustrated. This did not bode well for the entire ghetto population. The bloodthirsty Nazi had wanted to practice his sharpshooting on me, but I'd escaped the net. What would stop him from trying out his gun on the next Jewish child that he saw? Absolutely nothing.

Mama wasted no time. She sent all the children to the bunkers immediately.

"Sima," she said, "I am very concerned. The commandant is probably furious. He's going to want a child to slaughter. He's not used to losing."

Implicit in her words was the following dilemma: Was I willing to allow another child to be killed because of me? Or should I give myself up so that nobody else would get killed?

On the other hand, even if I gave myself up, the chances of the Germans satisfying their bloodlust solely on me were extremely slight. Even if I were to present myself to them, it would just mean that even more people would be killed.

I thought and thought, and decided that if I saw the Germans going house to house looking for the "little rabbit" that had managed to elude their fearless leader and willing to accept a replacement, then I would give myself up. I was not going to let some other child be killed because of me.

But then Mama considered the problem a little more, and she began shaking her head. She had calmed down and was speaking thoughtfully.

"Sima," she voiced her thoughts aloud, "if we knew that by giving yourself up, the Germans would take only you and nobody else, then giving yourself up would be an option. But truthfully, you and I both know that the Germans will laugh at your *ehrlichkeit* in coming out into the open—and then they'll use *both* captives for target practice."

In the end, the Germans didn't come looking for me and nobody had to give themselves up. For now.

This was our life, and these were the kind of dilemmas facing the residents of every ghetto on a day-by-day basis. There are even books of Halachic responsa from the ghettos of Poland that were assembled to deal with these horrifying issues. The unique questions that arose only in that pit of insanity known as the Holocaust.

I had already learned what commerce was all about. I had a solid grasp of the world of ghetto finance and business. I'd sold loaves of bread in Cracow, and cookies in Bregal. Now I decided to go into chocolate.

There was a method to the madness even in Bochnia. Every ghetto had gates where the Jews stood and placed orders, which were then filled by the local Polish gentiles. The gentiles delivered the goods when the Germans weren't looking, the Jews paid, and then the goods were resold for a profit.

I put in an order for chocolates.

It was wartime and chocolate was scarce, but the willing little gnomes that filled our orders through the very efficient black market delivered my chocolates within a short time. There was still money in the ghetto, and not a lot to do with it. Bread was scarce. All food was scarce. Which child—or adult, for that matter—could resist a delicious piece of chocolate?

Not many.

The chocolate went quickly. I made a tiny amount of profit on every deal. I used the profit to take one chocolate for myself.

Then I headed over to the house where Rivka lived.

———⋙◦⋘———

Rivka.

My beloved sister.

She had never recovered after that drenching ride through the sleet and the hail. These days, she was sicker than ever. She couldn't move from the special bed that Mama had somehow managed to get hold of for her.

I entered the house where Rivka lay from morning to night, as if waiting for death to come and whisk her away from us in its long, grasping arms. I entered my sister's sick room and looked at her through blurry eyes. This was Rivka. So close to me. I loved her so much. I couldn't bear to see her in such pain and discomfort. I wanted so much to help her be happy.

I'd come to give her a chocolate. It was the least I could do.

That day, for the first time in a very long time, my sister and I had a heart–to-heart talk. Who was going to make it through the war? Who would survive?

She was only fourteen.

"You will survive," she told me, her eyes glistening with unshed tears. "You will save yourself. I can feel it inside my heart." She delivered this line with somber finality, as if she could see into the future and knew things that others didn't.

She was quiet.

"I'm almost gone," she said at last, her eyes flashing with a hint of the old fire that had once been such an integral part of my Rivka. "There is no reason for me to eat. No reason for me to take away resources from others who have a chance of survival. I can't walk. I can't move. I will not take your chocolate. I refuse to deprive you of something that could give you a chance to survive."

I gave it to her anyway. I forced her to accept my gift of love.

But she didn't want it. Because she knew that she was already gone.

How she must have suffered as she waited for the end, knowing that it was only a matter of time until she was plucked from among us like a youthful flower that was never given a proper opportunity to bloom. For the rest of my life, whenever I was experiencing real joy, I thought of her. Of my sister Rivka, who never really had the chance to live.

She passed away in my mother's arms. From hunger.

There was simply nothing for her to eat. And, in any case, she'd wanted it to be finished already.

But that one time, when I brought her the chocolate that I had acquired through so much work, I made her promise that she would eat it, that she would partake of its goodness. That she would experience the joy and rich taste that had been a piece of our youth. And she agreed. She ate the chocolate.

But that happened only once. And it wasn't enough to stem the tide. In the end, she left us. She left me.

I miss her so much.

———❖———

Just before Purim, the Nazis came again.

It was time for another ghetto cleansing. Fortunately, Zeide Shaya'le wasn't in the ghetto just then. He'd been smuggled out of Bochnia and taken to Cracow until it was "safe" to return.

As mentioned previously, I wasn't the kind of child to stick around if the Germans were coming back. I was in no mood to be someone else's rabbit. Instead of taking my chances inside the ghetto, I decided to take my chances outside its walls.

Escaping wasn't difficult. There were more than enough holes in the ghetto gates. This wasn't Auschwitz or Treblinka. There were no huge, electric barbed-wire fences surrounding us. There was no need for them. The Germans knew that almost none of us would be able to survive on the outside for long.

Consequently, almost nobody was willing to take the risk.

But I was willing. I wasn't prepared to wait for them to come with their dogs and their guns and troop carriers filled with all those perfect specimens of German manhood. So I left.

My destination: the nearby train station.

I had no papers. No identification. Nothing to hide behind or to protect myself with. It was me and *Hashem* against the world.

I boarded a train, took a seat, and pretended that I had nothing to hide. The fact that I'd left a few days before the "*razzia*" was slated to begin helped me to pass undetected. My heart almost gave out every time a soldier walked past me, every time a policeman's eagle eyes took the measure of the carriage. Yet I held my head high and faced the world on my own terms. And I made it to Cracow without being stopped.

The next step was getting into the Cracow ghetto, which was a challenge as well, because it was just as hard to get into a Jewish ghetto as it was to get out. But *Hashem* was with me and I had perfect *mazal*. This time.

I stayed in my aunt's house in Cracow, while Zeide Shaya'le sheltered in a different relative's home in the ghetto. I remained for a few days, along with another cousin and his three children. His wife had already been killed by the Nazis. The house was full of the boisterous sounds of three lively children playing with one another. But I managed to witness something that shook even me, who had already seen so much.

One of the children had an abscess on her back. It was full of pus and needed medical care. My cousin, a *tzaddik* who knew nothing about tending to children and even less about medicine, did his best to care for his sweet little girl. What did he know? He knew how to learn, how to *daven*. But his wife was gone. It was up to him to take care of his children when they were ill. He had to place hot patches on his baby's sensitive back. He'd heat those patches up on the stove or the *blech* and then lay them as tenderly as he could on her back. But they were steaming hot, and her back was full of pus.

How that little girl screamed! You couldn't escape those cries of agony. They filled every room. And who could blame her? The pain was terrible, and she was just a baby. I will never forget the beatings that were inflicted on my fellow Jews, and I will also never forget the pain of baby Sara'le. How she cried — and we cried along with her.

Purim was about to arrive, and the Germans exited the Bochnia ghetto once again, leaving behind a heartbroken and much-diminished populace. It was safe to return now.

Going back meant taking a train from the Cracow station—a dangerous proposition in anyone's book. I had no papers. No band around my arm. I had absolutely nothing. I was a person with no right to exist.

And this time, my luck ran out. I was caught by the Germans.

I guess it had to happen sooner or later. I wasn't invisible, after all.

The crazed officer in charge of the Cracow ghetto was known far and wide by the nickname of Fore-Maruchki. "Maruchki" meant little or diminutive, and the word "fore" was derived from "foreman." The little foreman. He was a vicious, evil person with a vile temper. The little foreman couldn't let a day go by without murdering at least one Jew.

Shooting, hanging, or with his bare hands; how he did it wasn't as important as the fact that the deed was done. He would go to the ghetto or the factories, grab someone at random from a busy street or from a line of men hunched over their machines—and a shot would ring out. Fore-Maruchki was a sadistic, twisted creature, like so many of the Nazi leaders.

They caught me at the station, along with another girl

whose brother used to learn in my father's *yeshivah* back in the Sucha days.

We were standing on different parts of the platform, pretending that we did not know each other. The Nazis got us both. It wasn't difficult. We had no means of identification. No shield to hide behind. Not only that, but she had her eight-month-old niece with her, and that was a death sentence all by itself. A baby? How dare you shelter a Jewish child? That alone was deserving of death!

All around us, people were going about their business, laughing and talking, conducting their lives in the normal fashion. But for us, the game was up. I was just surprised it had taken them so long to get their claws on me.

We were caught by two soldiers on patrol. They were excited. Now they could cut the patrol short. They'd netted three Jews already; a pretty good haul for such a quiet day.

"Come along with us," they ordered. We followed them. What choice did we have?

There was a mini-police station in the train depot itself, making it all the easier for the Germans to catch as many Jews as possible. This was a long, rectangular room furnished with desks and metal file cabinets. Pictures of Hitler and other "great minds" hung on the walls. Officers were coming and going, making plenty of noise. All of them were smoking. A bluish cloud of hazy smoke hung over the room, drifting over the typewriters and up to the ceiling.

A small bench was parked against the side of the room. "Sit down and be quiet!" the soldiers barked at us.

We hadn't been planning on making any noise.

Truthfully, we were grateful that they'd allowed us to sit. Since when did Nazis allow Jewish children to sit down? A German soldier was standing right beside me, his gun aimed at the young enemies seated on the bench, as if he thought we were about to jump up, storm the room, and kill them all. What did they think we were going to do already?

We didn't look at each other.

I was even afraid to breathe. What would happen if I exhaled too loudly? Maybe the soldier would think I was trying to escape, and he'd shoot me. It was the most shallow breathing I've ever done. I'm positive the other girl felt the same way.

My mind raced. We'd been caught (she holding a baby!). There was no way out. We were finished. This was the den of Fore-Maruchki, personal emissary of the Angel of Death. We knew who he was and what he did. Everyone knew. There were no exit signs here. It was just a matter of time until they took us outside, stood us in front of a wall and gunned us down.

I had a silent conversation with *Hakadosh Baruch Hu*, begging Him to save us, and pleading with Him to make it quick and relatively painless if this was my time to go.

Across the room, one of the soldiers put in a call to the Little Foreman.

I held my breath.

The phone rang. Again. And then again. Finally, someone at the other end answered, and the soldier started to speak.

"Commandant," he said with a victorious grin, "we've caught two young girls, one of whom is holding a baby —"

This was as far as he got, when he was interrupted by raging screams coming from the other end of the line.

"DUM-KUP!! Idiot!! You stupid fool!" Fore-Maruchki was screaming at him with all his considerable lung power. "That's why you woke me up?! Can't I have a few minutes of rest without you stupid donkey soldiers calling me up and disturbing me? You caught Jewish girls? Big deal! I can go out and kill Jewish girls any time I want. How *dare* you!"

We heard him across the room. I wouldn't have been surprised if they heard him out in the station. The screaming was so loud that the soldier had to move the receiver away from his ear. He was literally shaking with fear. For once, the shoe was on the other foot. He knew how crazy Fore-Maruchki was. He knew full well what the Little Foreman was capable of. And now the commandant was furious with him.

"But, sir, what should I do with them?" The soldier's voice shook in panic.

From the other end of the line came more furious shouting.

"What should you do with them? I don't care. Give them a kick and throw them on the next train out of there! *That's* what you should do with them! Let them be someone else's problem. Just get rid of them! And don't *ever* wake me up again!"

It did my heart good to hear a Nazi trooper being berated like that. The young soldier who'd been guarding us took us back across the station and over to the train, making sure we were safely aboard! It was as if the Angel of Death himself had lifted me up out of harm's way and set me down, as tenderly as you please, right on the exact train that I needed to get out of the city.

The girl and her tiny charge took a seat at one end of the train and I found an empty seat on the other side. It was February, and freezing outside. The train was icy, but thankfully I had a coat. It was navy blue, and I was proud of it.

A Polish woman and her child took the seat across from me. I hate Polish women. To me, they represent the absolute dregs of humanity. In my experience they are some of the meanest people in the universe.

She was staring at me. I found this unnerving. Had she guessed that I was a Jew? And, if so, what was she going to do about it?

Suddenly she began to scream and point.

"Look, look everyone! Look at this Jewish girl running away from the ghetto! She has a bedbug on her coat! There's a bedbug on her coat. She must be a dirty Jew!"

Why did she have to scream like that? Why was she so happy that she had found me out? Why was she searching with her eyes for a German soldier? What was wrong with those Polish animals? The majority of the other passengers in the carriage were laughing along with her. Some of them were good Poles and laughing out of habit; some might just have been afraid *not* to laugh. But nobody came to our aid. Nobody said a word in our defense.

There was one man who looked at me with something akin to pity.

The women were worse than the men. Either they were enjoying our discomfort and fear, or they were pretending very well.

I sat rigid in my seat, wondering, *How many times can I be lucky enough to escape this madness? I just got away from the Little Foreman — but if another German comes along, I'm gone.*

Out of desperation, I did something crazy. Something extraordinary. Without a doubt, my actions came straight from *Hashem*.

I began laughing as well!

I began laughing, pretending that it was all a joke. That she was crazy. I was a gentile just like her, and she was crazy. I laughed and laughed. And felt terribly relieved when the kind Polish man who had been looking at me with such pity reached over and plucked the bedbug off my coat. And while I laughed, I prayed and prayed that no one else would walk into that carriage. And no one did.

When everything had calmed down and all the laughing Polish idiots had sunk back into their boorish stupor, I pretended that I was carsick and needed to throw up. I moved to the front of the train where there was a toilet, biding my time until that nightmarish journey had finally come to an end.

Eventually, the train began to slow down. I remained where I was, pretending to catch my breath after retching, but really keeping a sharp lookout for any approaching Germans. People were gathering their luggage as they prepared to disembark.

You can't wait until this train comes to a complete stop, I told myself. I knew that if I waited until the train entered the station, I would have to contend with that Polish witch, who would doubtless begin screaming for the Germans the second the train came to a complete halt. Every train station was crawling with Nazis. I would be caught yet again, and this time — I didn't even want to imagine the consequences.

There was only one thing to do.

I would have to jump before the train entered the station proper.

And that was what I did.

I stood poised in the space between the cars, on the short flight of stairs that would normally be used for alighting.

"*Hashem*, it's up to you. Please let me survive this!" I jumped.

I landed on my knees in a shallow ditch. Ignoring the intense pain, I waited for the train to pass me on its way into the station. And when it had finally moved on, I got up and ran—but not toward Bochnia. Instead I ran in the opposite direction, hiding in the fields and doing my best to remain inconspicuous as I made my way to a nearby village. I took off my coat to check if there were any more bugs. I saw some kids playing nearby, but did my best to stay away from them, waiting, waiting on a side street until evening, when I'd be able to leave this place and go back home.

As night fell, I returned to the tracks so I could get my bearings and find my way back to Bochnia.

I took my time. I had to make sure that Polish woman hadn't told anyone who would be lying in wait for me.

I stood silently in the shadows for a long time. I was in no rush. My life was the most important thing. Finally, I decided that the coast was clear and I could enter the ghetto.

It was the middle of the night.

Reb Shloma'le Bobover's house was built right up against the ghetto wall. I could have knocked on his door, but I didn't want to frighten his family at such an hour, even though they were my close relatives. Instead, I found my way between the holes in the ghetto wall and continued on inconspicuously toward home: the quintessential Jewish refugee, afraid of her own shadow.

That's how dangerous it was to take the train in those days.

———⊷•⊷———

I crept through the streets until I arrived at the front door. I pushed it open lightly. I didn't want to frighten anyone. My heart was overflowing with joy and gratitude to *Hakadosh Baruch Hu* for saving me, not once, but many times. All in the course of one journey. *Tefillas Haderech* had never been more meaningful.

They were sitting in the kitchen.

I walked into the warm, homey room. There might not have been much food, but a kitchen is still a kitchen. It was the room where everyone felt most comfortable sitting and talking. The moment I stepped through the doorway, they erupted.

"Sima! How was your trip?"

"What happened?"

"We were so worried about you! We heard about all the patrols at the Cracow train station!"

I sidestepped their countless questions. I wasn't ready to talk about the miracles I'd just experienced.

Eventually, everyone in the household got ready to go to sleep. It was the wee hours of the night and time to retire. Soon only Mama and I remained.

"Mama?"

"Yes?" She barely looked up from her sewing.

"A few miracles happened to me on the trip home."

"What do you mean, miracles?"

"Real, honest-to-goodness miracles. *That's* what I mean!"

Now she was staring at me, half in confusion, half in anticipation, with a little bit of worry thrown in for good measure.

"What exactly happened on your way back home?"

"I got caught on the platform of the Cracow train station."

"Caught?"

"The Germans caught me with no papers, along with another girl and her baby niece."

Mama turned pale. "What did they do?"

"They escorted us to the police station in the terminal."

"And. . ."

"And they held us at gunpoint while one of them called Fore-Maruchki on the telephone to inform him of their catch."

A dawning terror was forming in her eyes. Yet I glimpsed another emotion there as well.

"What did he do? How did you survive. . .? Fore-Maruchki? That butcher! How are you even alive?" There was wonder in her voice.

So I told her. I related the incredible tale of how my life had been saved because the Little Foreman had been woken up in the middle of his nap.

Mama did not use the words, "I don't believe you," but she did advise me not to share this story with anyone. And I understood that she was wondering whether I'd imagined the whole crazy story—because nobody who fell into Fore-Maruchki's clutches ever managed to escape. That just didn't happen.

Yet it *had* happened. It had happened to me.

My own mother didn't believe me. She told me to tell no one about my miraculous escape.

Some time later, a man came to visit us. He was sitting in the kitchen with Mama and they were talking. I don't remember what they were talking about. Then out of the blue, he asked the following: "Rebbetzin, wasn't it your daughter that was caught by Fore-Maruchki?"

Mama was speechless.

When she found her tongue, she asked, "Did Sima tell you that?"

"Absolutely not! I heard it through a different girl who was caught at the same time. You know, Rebbetzin, their survival was an amazing miracle. Truly miraculous! To get pulled into that madman's clutches and survive to tell the tale! She really should *bentch gomel* for this –" "Yes," Mama said wonderingly. "She really does have to *bentch gomel*."

For the first time, Mama actually believed that I had been telling the truth. It had been confirmed independently and she knew now that it hadn't been my imagination. She was infinitely grateful.

You have to understand: we never sat around and discussed these miracles, because they were a normal part of life for us. Anyone who managed to live through those crazy years didn't bother dwelling on every little point. It was enough that we were surviving. That was the main thing.

Dates and times? They meant nothing. What mattered to us was waking up in the morning, alive.

CHAPTER EIGHT

W E WERE JEWS. WE MAY HAVE BEEN PRISON-
ers, but we were still *Yidden*, and that wouldn't
change no matter what they did to us. Consequently,
we marked our time by the *Yamim Tovim* , just as we'd always
done. Our lives had turned upside down—but for a Jew, as
different as things get, somehow they are always the same.

Pesach time had arrived.

We weren't going to be celebrating in the style of the
past. Gone were all the china and crystal. Gone were the
bottles of ruby-red wine and the platters of delicious meat.
Golden chicken soup was a memory. *Charoses* would be an
entity comprised mainly of imagination. But we would still
be gathering for a *Seder*.

Zeide Shaya'le would recline at the head of the table, his
children and grandchildren surrounding him on all sides.
He'd relate the story of how the Halberstam family had
made it out of Mitzrayim (Egypt) thousands of years before,
and how we were hoping and *davening* with all our strength

for a similar salvation to take place once again. *"L'shanah Haba B'Yerushalayim"* had never held such meaning as it did when recited in a small house in the Bochnia ghetto, surrounded by German soldiers.

And there would be matzos. How did I know this? Because they were baked by the children of the ghetto, under the supervision of a few adults.

We rolled out the dough, and ran the heavy "roller" through each and every matzah, providing them with the requisite holes. We stuck those matzos in the makeshift oven for a few minutes, and then they were set aside to cool on a tray at the side of the room. For the most part, the adults kept out of the way. They were afraid to be involved, knowing what would happen should a Nazi patrol catch sight of the smoke rising from the oven. On the other hand, if it was just a bunch of youngsters —

In the end, we managed to bake a quantity of matzos which, although not large, was sufficient for our needs. Real matzos in the middle of the ghetto!

That was a *Seder* I will never forget. Pale, haggard faces and worn-down bodies that knew what it meant to work as we'd worked back in Mitzrayim, all seated around the holiday table. Of food, there may have been little to speak of. But the stories that Zeide told, the spiritual nourishment that we gleaned by listening to his holy lips tell the story of our ancestors, gave us hope that the story of freedom would be repeated once again in our own day as well.

There may not have been many matzos, but the glow on our faces gave the impression that we had baked enough for the entire ghetto. How I wish that I could say "Next Year in Jerusalem" now with the same passion I infused into those words back then!

———

Months passed. Months of daily miracles.

There came a point when the family had to split up again. It was a real feat that we had managed to remain together until then. But the ghetto had become a tiny place, now that the Germans had taken so many of us away. All the men of our family—all the Sanzer cousins, all the *eineklach*, all these descendants of the Divrei Chaim—moved into one apartment along with Zeide Shaya'le, the undisputed patriarch of the family. Meanwhile my mother, the girls, and my little brothers all moved into a different flat, a short distance away.

The Belzer Rebbe had been holding court in the Bochnia ghetto until he was smuggled out along with his brother-in-law and *gabbai*. Now that they had left, their apartment was empty. My Zeide moved the men of the family into it.

——————

The Jews of Czechoslovakia knew about Jewish Poland's imminent demise. It was only a matter of time before the Germans liquidated every single ghetto in every city and sent their inhabitants to the gas chambers. That was why the Czech Jews sent over men who knew how to smuggle people over the border.

But they needed a liaison in the ghetto. An address. In many cases, my mother served as that address. This would not only allow her to send her children out of the ghetto, but to assist many others in getting their children out as well.

For the last few months, we'd been hearing a litany of terrible news. The Cracow ghetto had been destroyed. Razed to rubble. Do you have any idea how it felt to hear that a beautiful, historical *kehillah* such as Cracow had been burned to the ground? It was a nightmare come true!

We heard about the heroic battle of the Warsaw ghetto, in which a handful of starving fighters fought off the might of the German Army for weeks with pipes and homemade bombs, using the tunnels and sewers of the ghetto and whatever ammunition they could find, purchase, or steal to hold off the enemy. But, in the end, the Warsaw ghetto was obliterated as well.

All this, despite the fact that the war was going badly on many fronts, and despite the fact that the trains of Europe could have been put to much better use for the war effort. But the Nazis didn't have time for the war. Every city's ghetto had to be taken over, resistance knocked down, and the Jews of the ghetto either killed on the spot or escorted to the trains for deportation to Auschwitz, to be turned into ashes and soap.

Bochnia was the last ghetto. We were the last ones left.

It was imperative that we escape in those final moments, before the Germans marched in to crush our homes, our families, and our fragile lives, once and for all.

I don't know how Mama was able to make contact with the Jews of Czechoslovakia, but suffice it to say, non-Jewish smugglers were put in touch with my family. It was time to get out of the burning building before the entire structure imploded before our eyes. My mother sent my siblings away with these smugglers. She sent the Vizhnitzer grandchildren as well, going so far as to even send a boy who had been born in 1942 and was only one year old. Many of these children made it as far as Budapest, where they eventually fell into German hands and were sent back to Poland to be killed.

I know that one is not supposed to travel during the "Nine Days." One is definitely not supposed to travel on the fast of the Ninth of Av itself. But when it's a matter of life or death—that's a different story. We had to leave, and *Tishah B'Av* was the night.

But before I left the ghetto with the peasant smuggler, I was brought to Zeide Shaya'le's apartment to say goodbye to the most loving grandfather the world has ever known. To bid farewell to the one who was probably the most important figure in my life — to this very day.

———⊷•⊶———

A few words about *Tishah B'Av* in the ghetto.

Do you know what it means to be sad? Do you know sadness?

That night was sadness in its purest form. As if someone had been able to bottle a pure distillation of the emotion called "sadness."

The night of *Tishah B'Av* was always an extremely powerful time, made all the more so by the fact that we were spending it under the ever-watchful gaze of the Nazi sadists. The Vizhnitzer Rebbe, Rav Baruch Chaim Rubin, was with us for the reading of *Megillas Eichah* and reciting *Kinnos*.

We had a *Tishah B'Av* tradition that involved potato sacks.

All of us were sitting on the floor. The floor was filthy, but not even remotely as dirty as the sacks that we kept in our home, which had been filled with potatoes and the ever-present dirt from the potato fields that came along with them. Every adult in the room took a turn draping his or her head with those sacks. Making themselves filthier then they already were. Then it was our turn. Every child draped his or her head with the sacks, allowing the dirt to cascade over our bodies. Then we were instructed to bang our heads against the cast-iron stove.

A good *klap*.

They wanted us to know what *Tishah B'Av* was really all about.

I recall all the explanations. We were told how what we were going through now was just like what our ancestors went through back in Jerusalem, thousands of years earlier.

History was repeating itself, and this time it was we who were to be the *korbanos* on the altar. There had been a *churban* then, and there was another one taking place now.

Just as Jerusalem had been blotted out by the Romans, the entire world of European Jewry was being methodically decimated by the Germans.

———————

I traversed the silent ghetto streets, apprehensively glancing at every shadow, every weed or blade of grass that moved in the summer-night breeze. The Germans had not yet arrived, but they might be here at any moment. Had I made it this far, only to see my freedom snatched away at the last second?

I wanted to leave the ghetto. I couldn't wait to leave the ghetto! But there was thing I needed to do first. And that was to say farewell to my Zeide.

Zeide Shaya'le was standing in the room he used as a study. He was truly old by then. Stooped. Bent over. A shadow of his former self. Yet from his eyes flashed a fire that reminded me of the man he'd been in younger years. It showed me that the Zeide I'd always known and loved was still in there somewhere.

He looked at me questioningly.

"Simchah'le?"

"Yes, Zeide."

"Did the Belzer Rebbe leave yet?"

He must have known that the Belzer Rebbe was long gone. Maybe he'd forgotten. He was very old.

"Yes, Zeide. The Belzer is long gone."

The room was still, the mustiness redolent with the scent of tea and *sefarim, sefarim, sefarim*. The holy books that he loved with all his heart. Even now, some of them were open on the table.

Zeide Shaya'le stepped out of himself then.

"You will go *b'shalom*, in peace," he whispered in a trembling voice. "You, Simchah'le, will be saved. You will live."

Everything he said sounded like a prophecy of old, and *Der Zeide* himself seemed like a *navi* of old.

The next words he uttered shocked me to my very core.

"Your mother and your father — they will not survive —"

Alarmed, I pulled back. I didn't want to hear these awful predictions. But I felt a compulsion to continue asking him, pressing him for what the future held.

"And *Der Zeide*? Will you live?"

My voice was tremulous—the voice and manner of a little child seeking reassurance from someone he trusts and receiving none, because there is no reassurance to give.

And Zeide raised his finger, and he said, "*Nein, mein kind.* (No, my child.)"

"Only I will survive?" (*Ribbono shel Olam*, how horrible a fate: to be the sole survivor of such an illustrious family!)

"No, you will not be alone. But the majority will not survive."

There we stood, together and yet alone. Zeide Shaya'le and his beloved granddaughter. The smell of a wax candle filled the air as it slowly suffocated to death in the almost airless chamber.

I began to cry. Zeide Shaya'le was shedding tears, too. It was the only time in my life that I saw my Zeide cry.

We began moving toward the window. He was talking to me and shuffling over to the window at the same time—the one that looked out at the ghetto partition. Zeide moved the paper curtain aside just a tiny bit. It was pouring outside.

The rain was coming down as if someone had opened a gigantic faucet and was letting it run until the world below was drowned in the flood. The water hit the windowpane, sizzling downward with incredible force. Far off in the distance, thunder boomed. A jagged edge of lightning slashed the bloated sky with intense savagery. There we stood, crying together, and Zeide said, "*Zeist, mein kind, inz veinin. In himmel veint mein mit inz.*" (See, my child, we're crying. In Heaven they're crying along with us.)

It was the most terrifying moment in my entire life.

Just then my father entered the room and said, "Sima you have to leave now. *Schnell.* Fast. Right away!" There was an urgency in his voice that could mean only one thing.

Germans.

I took my Zeide's hand in mine and I kissed him good-bye.

Then I left the room, shoulders heaving, despair in my heart.

How we loved that man! Such a wonderful, loving person.

So do you think that only we cry—that the Heavens themselves don't know how to shed a tear? I can assure you that they do. They know how to cry far better then we'll ever know.

———

Mordechai Giewirtik was a poet who lived in Cracow. He summed up our lives in a few terse lines that rang of truth and suffering.

> *We lie there, our terror grows,*
> *When a door creaks,*
> *Our hearts quake when a mouse,*
> *Starving, nibbles paper.*
> *So we lie there, filled with terror*
> *Suffering, denigrated like slaves,*
> *And so our days drag on,*
> *And so our sleepless nights.*

That was exactly the way it was.

This is not to say that everyone was afraid of the Germans. There were Chassidim all over Poland, in every ghetto, who stood up straight and didn't cower. People who didn't shave even one hair of their beards, who looked the Nazis in the eye and laughed at them. Their leader was a young man named Matisyahu, who was originally from a non-religious, completely assimilated family from Vienna, and who rejected every ideal he'd been brought up with to learn Torah at Yeshivas Chachmei Lublin under the guidance of Rav Meir Shapiro. Under Matisyahu's leadership, bands of youth were formed that cared nothing for the German regime. They were not the slightest bit fearful of death. They hid and learned and survived on nothing. They laughed in death's face and danced at the edge of the pits as the machine-gun fire pierced them through.

Ana avda di'kudsha brich hu! I am the servant of *Hakadosh Baruch Hu!* That was the mantra.

They were not afraid. But I didn't have the backing of such a group, or their Torah learning and fiery *Chassidus* to fall back on. I was a little girl leaving her Mama and Tatte — and her Zeide — to rush out of our house before the Nazi soldiers came calling for me. I had to creep along the shadowy walls lining the muddy streets, seeking the cracks and holes that would allow me to slip away unnoticed from the few narrow streets that were all that remained of the ghetto, and escape into the giant world beyond.

I was headed for Baratska 5.

Our erstwhile home. Now home to someone else. Someone still loyal to our family. Someone with foreign documents who was legally allowed to reside outside the ghetto walls. Someone who was willing to shelter a young girl in the attic until the gentiles arrived to take her away.

And so, I left the ghetto to take up residence in my

temporary place of refuge, where every knock meant the Germans had come to seize me at last, and every creak was a sign of the enemy's approach. As I huddled under heaps of blankets and straw, my imagination sent a series of terrifying pictures to my sleep-addled brain. Pictures of soldiers waiting below and dogs straining at their leashes. Soldiers and dogs coming to take me away, to the train station where the cattle cars wait patiently —

This was my life.

———

A few days passed in this fashion. And then, one day, I heard feet climbing the ladder up to the attic.

I stood trembling in a far corner of the room. The trap door opened up, and my host was standing in the doorway. There was a cheerful expression on his face.

Probably because I was about to leave.

"Your mother has managed to acquire the necessary documents for herself, you, and your siblings to live outside the ghetto," he told me.

I sense that he was leaving out much more then he was telling me.

"What about papers for my Tatte?" I shouted. "What about papers for Zeide Shaya'le?"

There was a look of infinite sadness in his eyes. He knew that I was not shouting at him, but rather at the world in general, a world that makes people choose who will live and who will die. But he was helpless to do anything about any of this. He could only hand me a package of food and watch me put my meager belongings together as I waited for nightfall, so I could go join what remained of my family in the non-Jewish part of town.

———

Now we were "safe."

We were living outside the ghetto, under the very noses of the Nazis. In the actual backyard of the Polish beasts. Our minds however, were still with those who had been left behind in the last few, ever-shrinking streets of the Bochnia ghetto. My Tatte. My Zeide. Both of them still learning with all their might. Still trusting in *Hashem* with all their hearts.

Mama had somehow acquired a loaf of bread. It was a small loaf, easily hidden under a coat. Something that a child such as myself would have no problem transporting to the ghetto.

We knew what was happening in the world we'd left behind. They were literally starving in those bullet-riddled homes. Pinched-faced people, praying, crying, begging for a piece of bread, for anything to eat. And here I had an entire loaf nestled beneath my coat, waiting to be passed through the fence, handed over with love to my Tatte who'd be waiting for me.

I left Baratska 5 with trepidation. The warm loaf felt like a bomb against my body. If I was caught by the Germans I would be shot on the spot, with no questions asked. I was literally shaking from head to toe. I tremble now as I recall that walk. Baratska 5 was not far from the ghetto walls. But as close as it was, it was a world away.

Every step I took was calculated. Every movement was designed to keep me safe. Soon I was stepping through a gap between two houses. I could see the ghetto walls, so close.

Tatte would be waiting there. My beloved Tatte would be standing at the designated spot, and I would run up to him and throw the loaf of bread over the fence. And he would catch it, and kiss me with his eyes, and whisper words of blessing even as he turned and ran and I turned and ran, fleeing for our lives in case anybody had witnessed the criminal act that had occurred right outside the Bochnia ghetto. He would hold that bread in his hands, cradling it as if it was gold, as if it was the most wonderful treasure in the universe. And then — Zeide Shaya'le would have something to eat.

I was about to begin the short walk (short in distance, but endless in the knowledge that every step could be my last) to the fence where Tatte was waiting—when I saw them.

They were just sitting there. German soldiers, leaning casually against a garden post, making conversation. They could have been discussing the state of the war, their fear of battle, the wives and children back home. But they were sitting right there. There was no way that I could get that loaf of bread to my Tatte!

Do you know what agony means? This was agony. I pictured my father starving. Tears coursing down his sunken cheeks. *Der Zeide* starving in the wooden house, his *sefarim* his only solace, ignoring the physical pain as he immersed himself in that which he loved most in the world. I could see the soldiers talking, and I could see Tatte standing there, and I couldn't approach. Because if I walked any closer—even just a little bit—they would see me, and it would all be over.

But that loaf of bread was burning a hole in my pocket!

Tatte couldn't see the Germans. The Germans couldn't see him.

But I could see both of them.

And I couldn't move.

If I came any closer I was afraid that they'd see me. Or him. What a terrible, terrible decision for a child to have to make. I just stood there, hoping that my father would go. That he wouldn't make any sign that would show the Germans he was there—because, if he did, out would come those guns. The soldiers would aim and fire, and then my Tatte would collapse on the ground, the life taken from him.

But he was watching me. He didn't know why I wasn't

moving. He was a smart man, but he just couldn't figure out why his daughter wasn't coming any closer. And I understood that as long as I stood there with that bread under my jacket, he would stand there, too. Waiting. Hoping.

I couldn't even wave to him or make any other sign, either of affection or warning. There was another street behind me, and gentiles were passing back and forth. If anyone noticed a little girl waving to a man with sad eyes behind the ghetto wall —

I couldn't breathe. What was I to do? What a challenging decision!

My father was watching me. There was a puzzled and hurt look on his face. He couldn't see the entire picture. He had no idea that there were Germans a few feet away from him. I was desperately afraid that he would call out. I couldn't even move.

You have papers in your pockets. Why are you so afraid? I asked myself.

Those aren't even your own papers. I responded angrily. *They belong to your cousin who escaped to Hungary, and they won't get you far if the Germans stop you and start with their questioning:*

"Why are you standing near the ghetto wall?

"Who gave you that loaf of bread, and who are you delivering it to?

"Who is your contact in the ghetto?"

They would accuse me of being a spy, and then nothing would be able to help me. I would be lost forever!

To my eternal pain and shame, I turned around and left. I walked away from that impossible situation and returned to my mother.

The memory haunts me to this very day. Seeing his confused, hopeless face recede behind me as he watched his little Sima turn around and leave with the life-giving sustenance beneath her coat. Any time I see bread, I remember what I did. Any time I'm about to sit down and have something to eat, I remember how I left them, how I abandoned them. And worst of all—how they didn't even know why.

I'm so sorry, Tatte. But what was I to do?

And the worst part of it all was that my dear, dear Tatte would never even know why his darling daughter had left them to starve.

———◦◦———

Mama spoke to me before I left Bochnia for the last time. My older sister Devora had already been smuggled out. The family was breaking apart into so many pieces, splintering in every direction. We sat together in the kitchen. Mama peered into my eyes as she spoke, trying to convey the seriousness of what she had to say.

"You are about to leave us."

I nodded, trying my hardest not to cry.

"I don't know if I will ever see you again, my darling daughter. But, *mein kind*, I need you to promise me that you will never forget where you come from. From which tree, which roots. You are a Sanzer *einikel*. A great-granddaughter of the holy Divrei Chaim of Sanz. You must never forget this great privilege. Treasure it. Be proud of who you are and don't become afraid by what is happening around you. And if you are scared, if you feel like you are in any danger at all, all you need to do is say '*Shema Yisrael*' and *Hashem* will help you."

Then Mama gave me a kiss. All her love for me was encapsulated in that kiss. That was the last time I saw my mother. The last time I saw Shea and Baruch. Shea, such a little *tzaddik*. And Baruch, so handsome, such a *mentsch*. I miss them so, so much!

———◦◦———

After that,, events began moving with dizzying speed. All I wanted was to curl up in bed, go to sleep, and wake up when it was all over. Instead there came a knock on the door that night, summoning me. It was time for me to leave. I was going with a farmer who moonlighted in smuggling people over the border and into safer, better lands.

He was tall and silent. Taciturn. Unyielding. He radiated a certain trustworthy, reliable power, like a solid oak tree. He hefted my bag in his powerful hands as if it weighed nothing, and set off. I waved goodbye to my siblings and my mother and then I followed him off into the darkness, trying to keep up with the fast clip of his long legs.

This man would now become my world. I would have to turn to him with any problems that I had. He would take care of me until we reached a place where other Jews could take over. I had no way of knowing whether he meant to betray me. No way of knowing what *Hashem* had in store for me. But Zeide Shaya'le's final words to me reverberated through my mind: *You will go in peace. You will be saved. You will live —*

It was Zeide's promise, and it was good enough for me.

<hr/>

We put the house in Bochnia behind us. The taste of finality everywhere. I was leaving everyone I loved. Snatches of my last conversation with Zeide flooded my mind. He had literally promised me that I would survive. Yet he had foretold the death of so many others.

Mama.

Tatte.

Himself.

"You will make it." How had he known? How *could* he have known? Did he have *ruach hakodesh*? I knew he was a *tzaddik*, but to be able to predict the future at such a time—

that was more than incredible —

It was difficult to ponder and run at the same time. My escort's legs were much longer and accustomed to walking quicker than mine were. I put aside my thoughts. I'd think later. Now I concentrated on keeping up with the farmer who'd come for me. He walked with assurance, and I tried to borrow some of it for myself. Confidence. Belonging. Ease. These were the feelings that were invaluable in times like this. In no time we had left Bochnia behind us and were headed toward the countryside.

The Polish countryside. So innocent in appearance, and yet raging under the surface with a bloodthirstiness so intense as to make any semblance of goodness fade into oblivion. The farmer was an outdoorsman. He knew all the shortcuts. It wasn't long before we were turning into a farm. I saw whitewashed buildings, log cabins, herds of sheep and other animals, and fields. Rolling fields. That's where we were headed. Straight for the middle of a far-off wheat field.

We walked through the field, the tall wheat bobbing and weaving in the gentle wind, the sun beginning its descent over the golden scene. So peaceful. So deceptive. Didn't I know that a bucolic scene like this could turn into a blood-bath in a matter of seconds?

We reached what seemed to be the absolute center of the field. The wheat was almost ripe, tall stalks towering above my head. The man bade me sit. Not to make a sound. Not to stand up. No one was allowed to see me. We were off the beaten track. There was nobody coming to work the fields at this hour. "Just stay down," he grunted, "and everything will be fine."

Then he left. Within moments, his sturdy, muscled body had been swallowed up among the wheat stalks. I was on my own. Condemned to wait in silence for my "savior" to return. I didn't know if he even would. I didn't truly know if he could be trusted. But I knew that I had no choice. So I waited there until nightfall.

It was the middle of the night when I heard the two Germans on patrol. I peered through the wheat stalks at the soldiers walking nonchalantly alongside the field, the sound of their guttural voices rising up on the cool night air, their laughter bringing back terrible memories of other encounters with their peers. My heart began beating faster. Would they leave the outer perimeter of the field and trample through the crops? Had they received information from an informer that there was a Jewish child hiding deep within all that wheat?

I watched fearfully.

They took their time. They were in no rush. Why should they be? They were Germans, and Germans let no detail, large or small, slip by them. There was some farm machinery left by the Polish farmers at the edge of the field. The soldiers sauntered over to the tracker. One lit up a cigarette, took a puff, gave a cough. The other climbed up the few shallow steps, took a look inside, saw that it was empty. There was nothing here for them. It wasn't long before the field was as empty as it had been before.

After they left, I lay facedown among the fragrant wheat and allowed my heart to slowly catch up with the rest of me. Gradually, the rapid pounding ceased and my breathing became less ragged. It had been close. Not that close, but close enough.

When would this nightmare end?

I had no way of knowing that this was just the beginning.

At some point in the night, the farmer emerged from the

darkness. He motioned me to follow him without a word. Through the slumbering wheat and past a pile of cut wooden logs waiting to be used for firewood. Up a short staircase and into a house, where I was once again directed to the attic and ordered to hide under a huge pile of hay, corn, and assorted vegetables that the farmer kept there, probably for camouflage.

Two days passed in this way. Two days of waiting. And then, toward evening, the smuggler brought another girl from the Bochnia ghetto into the attic. It was one of the Landau girls. Liba Landau, only five or six years old. And her joining my escape, the fact that I would now have to watch over a girl who was little more than an infant, would turn an already extremely arduous journey into something almost unbearable.

CHAPTER NINE

WE LEFT THE COMFORT AND RELATIVE SECU-
rity of the attic in the middle of the night, and
stepped back into the wilds of the dangerous
world, filled with wild beasts, Nazi soldiers, Polish peasants, informers, thieves, smugglers, policemen, and partisans of many nationalities who sometimes shot on sight and
didn't even pause to ask questions afterward.

Once we began the hike, we didn't stop. We walked and
we walked and walked. Through forests whose towering
trees made the night seem darker than it was possible to get,
and fields that seemed to stretch to infinity; over bridges
that spanned magnificent bodies of water which we could
barely see, and hills whose peaks seemed to touch the sky.
Europe is huge, and we were crossing it on foot.

At first, it was all right. We were moving, and the farther
we got from the Bochnia killing grounds, the better I felt.
But after a few kilometers, with the underbrush cutting into
my legs and the nettle bushes scraping us as we plowed

determinedly through their cutting edges, my feet began to complain. If at first they gave out slight murmurings of discontent, they soon began to throb. And then blisters began to form. After another ten kilometers, the blisters popped open and pus began to ooze, as the skin became raw and red and my feet asked me in innocent disbelief what they had done to deserve such horrible treatment.

And all that marching was done in complete silence; at least on my part. I gritted my teeth and marched. But the same could not be said for little Liba Landau, who had regretted agreeing to leave her mother from the second she'd been smuggled out of the ghetto. She was still a baby. Six years old. How could any six-year-old be expected to understand that she had to march until her feet were raw and her entire body ached?

She couldn't understand. She wanted to return to the ghetto, and her Mama.

It was all we could do to keep her from screaming.

The silent smuggler grabbed her hand and pulled her along. He was a powerful man with a fearful grip, and he didn't let go for a second. Liba's feet barely touched the ground. She was flying along over hill and dale while I scrambled to keep up with them both. After hours of nonstop hiking, the ground began to curve slightly upward as we started to ascend. If the going had been tough before, I soon realized that only now were we really starting to get serious. Every so often the pressure of the climb would increase for a while, until it leveled off. Soon we were all breathing heavily.

It was pure torture.

I was sweating from the exertion and freezing from the dampness, my clothes sticking to me, my breath coming in ragged gasps, and my heart beating rapidly, begging my brain for a break. But how could I do that, when I knew that it was imperative that we increase the distance between ourselves and Bochnia? Finally, just when I thought that if we went any further, any further at all, I would surely die, the farmer stopped. We had ascended high enough for one evening. He motioned for us to sit down. My shaky legs just gave in.

We collapsed in an exhausted heap on the ground, shuddering from the exertion.

"How much ground did we just cover?"

"Thirty-five kilometers," the farmer grunted.

I couldn't believe my ears. How does anyone cover thirty-five kilometers, much of it uphill, in a single night? Especially if you are a starved ghetto child of eleven accompanied by a girl of six who won't even lift her legs by herself! It was nothing short of miraculous.

We rested for only a short while, because we were still in the open, not far from the frontier, and this was a very dangerous place to just relax. We needed to hide. The farmer motioned for us to get up again, that it was time for us to begin moving toward the concealment of the forest. At that moment, we heard a sound that made the hairs on our arms and the back of our necks stand up in panic.

A German patrol was closing in on us!

We could hear the Nazi soldiers speaking as they climbed, the sound of their boots distinct on the hard-packed earth. They conversed in low guttural tones, banter and laughter merging with the sound of their guns slapping against their legs. This was a border patrol, and that meant that we were in serious trouble. Border troops were real soldiers, well-trained and rigid killing machines.

The farmer turned to me.

"You're in charge of the six-year-old. Tell them that your father left you alone and that you went looking for him, and that's how you got lost. Be convincing!"

I never saw someone disappear as quickly as that man. He simply vanished.

Evaporated.

And there we were, unprotected, with no documents and barely a cover story to use. A most unenviable position.

Mama's words came back to me.

"You are a Sanzer *einikel*. A great-granddaughter of the holy Divrei Chaim of Sanz. You must never forget this great privilege. Treasure it. Be proud of who you are and don't become afraid by what is happening around you. And if you are scared, if you feel like you are in any danger at all, all you need to do is say '*Shema Yisrael*' and *Hashem* will help you."

It was time to activate my secret weapon, just as Mama had said.

Our guide was gone. I looked down at my six-year-old charge, and then around at my surroundings. We needed a hiding place immediately. There was a gigantic tree nearby, with branches that spread overhead like a wedding canopy.

"Get behind that tree," I hissed.

She obeyed unquestioningly.

"Whatever happens now, you have to be smart. You hear me?"

She nodded.

"If the soldiers start walking around the tree trunk from one side, you slowly and quietly slide around to the other side. Make sure they don't see you."

Now what? I could hear the soldiers clearly. They were almost upon us. There was no time for me to find another hiding place. In sheer desperation, I threw myself behind another tree, but this one's trunk was not nearly as thick and even I, as skinny as was possible to be, didn't imagine that it would hide my entire body.

I also had another problem. I truly had no idea from

which direction they were coming. I could hear their voices being carried on the wind, and I could picture them in my mind's eye. But I wasn't sure where they would make their grand entrance.

So I lay down on the ground. Eyes open. Watching to see what was going to happen.

A few seconds later, the ground shook from their heavy tread. There I was, completely vulnerable on the ground, half-obscured by the tree that I'd crawled behind, my feet sticking out into the open, sure that the Germans would see me and raise their rifles. And then there would be a gigantic explosion, and that would be the end.

Just say "Shema Yisrael" — My secret weapon.

The patrol walked up the hill, conversing in low, rumbling tones, eyes shifting from side to side as they searched for illegal refugees trying to cross the border.

They are going to step on your legs! a tiny voice in my head screamed in panic.

I think my heart literally stopped beating for a few seconds.

And then — the soldiers stepped *over* my legs.

Not one of them.

All of them.

The entire patrol.

Stepped over my legs just as politely as can be. Not a single one of them noticed that they were in the presence of an eleven-year old criminal. True, I was wearing a dark coat, and yes, it was late at night. And yet, all it would have taken was for one of them to look down at the ground. They wouldn't have been able to miss me!

"*Shema Yisrael,*" I whispered.

I could feel them stepping over me! But they couldn't see me.

They had eyes, but they could not see.

Eventually the patrol passed us by and continued on into the mountains.

Liba came out from behind the huge oak. She wanted to know who those bad men were, and why I was afraid of them, and why I was shaking so badly. And then the gentile farmer reappeared. Without showing any emotion, he informed us that it was time to move on.

We left the place of our miracle. Our guide saw me still shaking and whispered that it was O.K. now, the danger had passed, we were all right.

"Don't worry, it's not far."

He was right. It wasn't far.

We followed him once again as he stepped across the brittle branches and forest foliage, sure footed and confident, in his element, barely making any noise despite his big size. We came to a series of little streams, which we crossed, and soon enough we were very deep in the woods.

"I will leave you now and return in the morning. You will be fine here." Then he was gone.

The middle of a Polish forest.

A few years earlier, I would have been petrified to find myself stranded in the middle of a pitch-black forest at three in the morning, but now I found that it didn't disturb me at all. How fascinating we humans are. How interesting and compelling a concept it was, that I'd rather be exposed to the wild animals of the forests and mountains than forced to share the world with the people who inhabited it. Animals killed because they needed to. People, on the other hand —

He'd left us not far from another stream. We could hear it gurgling as it rushed swiftly and purposefully over the rocks.

"You're going to want to approach that stream," he'd

warned us before taking his leave. "But it's not a good idea. Yes, you are in the middle of the forest, but there are workers here even now, during the night, and they, too, like the stream. So do yourselves a favor and stay away. I will return this evening."

We were going to have to remain by ourselves the entire day. Part of me was happy for the company that Liba provided, but the more practical part of me was extremely worried about how I was going to entertain this child and keep her from doing the kind of things that would give us away. It was still the middle of the night, but the sky was becoming a little rosier now, although actual light would not arrive for a while.

There we stayed, in a hidden alcove surrounded by powerful trees that stood guard like ancient sentries. Before we'd left the house, the farmer had handed me a basket with about two kilos of tiny pears. That was all the food we'd had from the time we'd set out walking until now. We were expected to make a thirty-five-kilometer hike with just some pears to eat! And the basket of pears was supposed to last us the entire next day as well. We were starving! But this was all we had.

I'd feared Liba was going to be trouble from the second I'd set eyes on her, and she quickly showed me how accurate my reading of her had been. She began to complain. She could hear the Polish workers talking to one another, and it frightened her.

When I whispered to her that if she didn't settle down and keep still, they would come and get us and then we'd probably be killed, she shrugged, cried, and told me in a biting tone of voice that if that happened, at least she'd be with her mother again. How was I supposed to respond to that? I, too, would have loved to be with my parents again, but something inside my soul was pushing me to run. Constantly.

I couldn't sleep, exhausted though I was, because I was afraid Liba would decide to go for a little stroll over to the workers or the stream. I'm sure that whoever those workers were, whether Jews or gentiles, there was definitely a German or two there to watch them. There was no way I was going to allow Liba to endanger us both. So I didn't sleep. And I didn't allow us to go drink at the stream, despite the fact that we had a ruinous thirst by then. Our throats were parched, and we felt sick from all the hiking. But our lives came first.

So we sat there the rest of the night without moving from our places, and through the entire day that followed. I would like you to ask yourselves whether you know any six-year-olds who are capable of behaving this way? The answer obviously is no. No six-year-old can do this. But she had no choice, and I guess she had internalized this fact in some part of her sub-conscious mind because she didn't try to disobey me. I stayed up to make sure that everything was as it should be.

No drinking.

No sleeping.

Only pears to eat. One at a time. Because we didn't know how much longer we were going to have to walk. Our stomachs were growling in distress and dismay, and we were crying, but we knew that it would be much worse to finish everything now and have nothing at all for later. So we controlled ourselves, even though we were only eleven and six years old.

The next night we set out again, eager to get far away from where we'd been hearing those workers conversing all the time, and hoping that at some point in the near future we'd finally be able to drink as much as we liked. At the end of the next evening's hike, we found ourselves once again near a stream, but this time it was located on the grounds of a house. Our farmer/guide left us again. But not for long. Soon enough he was back, and he was carrying a deep, very large bowl that was filled to the brim with potato soup! There was also one wooden spoon. But really, who needed a spoon?

Let me tell you something. I have never forgotten that potato soup. That soup was like something straight out of *Olam HaBa*. It was the best soup I have ever eaten. Even now, if I ever have the opportunity to enjoy a bowl of potato soup, it conveys the feeling of being full after a terrible starvation. To me potato soup, no matter how it tastes, is gold. Pure gold.

Liba got to use the spoon.

She was six years old and had to have her way. What was I supposed to do? Begin fighting with her over the spoon? Absolutely not. I would have given her anything, to make sure she didn't complain or threaten to run away. If being the one to use the spoon made all the difference, then it was absolutely worth it.

So she used the spoon, and I used my hands. It's not so easy to eat soup with your hands, even potato soup, but when you've just trekked for twenty-four hours with nothing to eat but some pears, the presence or absence of a spoon is not going to make much of a difference. I ate that soup using my hands as a spoon, and was happier than I'd been in a very long while.

The soup was nice and hot and it filled us up, and for a long time all we did was enjoy that soup. Eventually, the farmer returned to the house and brought another spoon. That soup would serve us well, because it gave us tremendous strength to continue.

After we finished eating, it was time to move again.

A few more hours of walking—made much easier due to the fact that we were full of potatoes—and we eventually reached another area where there were a number of farmhouses. This was quite a dangerous place to be, because by now we were very near the Czechoslovakian border.

"The frontier is very close by," our guide whispered hoarsely.

I was filled with radiant joy at this news.

Separating the Polish side of the border from the Czechoslovakian side was a huge river. We could see Czechoslovakia, we could even smell Czechoslovakia, but we knew that actually getting there was going to be difficult. The river was very deep, with a rapid current shifting downstream and sending branches and debris in all directions. The noise it made served as a warning that this was not a stream and not to be taken lightly.

Our silent guide lifted Liba in his arms. I climbed onto his back, and that was the way we began to cross the river.

I could barely keep my head above the frigid water as he strode through the current, his powerful arms, forging a way through the river. "Be still," he told Liba in his deep voice. He had his eye on the far bank, little Liba in his arms and me clinging to his broad back, as the current did its best to pull me off and send me downstream, never to be seen again. But I hadn't come this far to allow the river to get the better of me. I held on to that back with all my might and concentrated on keeping my head above the water. Closing my eyes, I imagined my mother's words flowing through my mind.

If you are ever scared, all you need to do is say "Shema Yisrael" —

The river might be roaring all around me, the man saving me may be a stranger who owed me less than nothing, but all that made no difference because I was in the hands of *Hashem*. If He wanted me to survive, I would. It didn't matter if a crazed Lagerfuhrer was using me for target practice in the Bochnia ghetto, or a German patrol was stepping over my legs in the depths of a Polish forest. It made no difference if Fore-Maruchki's boys caught me in the Cracow train station or if I was passing through a rushing river that was doing its utmost to disengage me from my guide's back. Nothing mattered, other than the will of *Hashem*. If He so desired, I would make it through all of this, and so would Liba.

Finally, we got across the river.

Then our guide grew very serious.

"The Germans are all around us now," he cautioned. "You must be completely still. No talking at all."

We had crossed the river, but there was still a little more walking to do before we would actually arrive in Czechoslovakia. Our taciturn guide's eyes darted everywhere, in every direction. He was alert, every sense heightened.

We were freezing from our soaking in the river, and at the same time we were hot from all the walking—but the fact is, we weren't really feeling anything at all, because our only goal was to keep moving until we got completely away from the Germans. What we passed through along the way meant nothing at all.

Hardship meant nothing. Discomfort meant nothing. The main thing was to save ourselves, no matter how much it hurt.

We arrived at our next rest stop, a private home, not long after our harrowing river crossing. There our guide disappeared again—only to reappear with another two girls, a seven-year-old cousin of mine who was the granddaughter of Rav Boruch Vizhnitzer, a Gorlitzer and Sanzer *einikel*, and another girl who was all of four years old.

This terrified me!

Would she ruin everything?

But that four-year-old kid turned out to be the best of the bunch. Uncomplaining. Completely accepting and always cheerful. She, too, understood that we wanted to escape this accursed land more than anything and she made it her mission to do just that. She was more like me than I was. She was a truly heroic child. My hero.

(Recently, my cousin's son donated a *sefer Torah* to a *shul* in my neighborhood, and my cousin made sure that I was invited so that all of the extended family could finally be together. There I was, talking to all of my cousins, when someone introduced me to a woman whom I hadn't seen since the war. Since our time together in the mountains and rivers of the Czechoslovakian frontier, in fact. My little heroine had survived the war. Oh, the catching up we had to do! She didn't remember any of the details. What do you expect? She was only four!)

———⟫•⟪———

All four of us hid in one room. There was a nice big bed in that room, covered in what was called a "pooch." A "pooch" is the type of thick, down-filled quilt that one ideally needs in order to thrive in a European winter. They are the warmest, coziest blankets in the world, ingenuously designed to help you forget what the weather is up to outside your toasty bedroom. The four of us stayed in very close proximity to the bed, the plan being that if anyone with evil intent should approach the house, we would quickly dive underneath the thick blanket that would camouflage our presence.

Here was one house where the lady of the manor took care of us and gave us food. We were warm, we had the most amazing blanket, there was sufficient food to eat, and everyone treated us nicely. This was like staying at the finest hotel.

But that night the Germans came to the village.

Our hosts were agitated and edgy. Maybe someone had seen our guide bringing all these girls to their house. So the Landau cousins were moved to a different location and our host brought Liba and me into the master bedroom to hide. She helped us lie down in her bed and draped her gigantic "pooch" over our shaking bodies, making sure it lay as smooth as possible so that that no one would be able to discern the shape of two little girls hiding beneath that quilt. After issuing a stern admonition for us not to cough, she left the room. We lay unmoving, not making the slightest sound.

It wasn't long before the dreaded knock arrived.

"Open up!"

"Who's there?"

"It's the German military police!"

The lady opened the front door and invited the German officers into her charming home. The house was quiet and peaceful, every item in its proper place, the tea kettle on the stove.

We could hear them talking through the bedroom door.

"Can I bring you officers a hot drink?"

"What did you have in mind?"

"How about a nice hot cup of tea with something a little stronger mixed in?"

"Sounds wonderful. It's really very cold outside, and my men would like nothing more than to get off the streets and back to their warm beds."

She assured them that she understood: a soldier's life was never easy. Soon enough they were seated at the kitchen table drinking big mugs of steaming tea, to which she'd added a generous dollop of brandy, while we lay still as statues under the blanket and tried not to breath. It felt like forever before they left, but eventually they finished their tea and bade her farewell without even entering the bedroom.

That was a lucky night for four girls who were attempting to cross the border.

———≫•≪———

Now that we were over the border, we'd hoped that our trials were over. But it seemed we were still fairly far away from our final destination. Our guide did not want us to have any contact with the Czechoslovakians, who would know that we were Polish refugees the moment we opened our mouths. Therefore, he kept us traveling on foot through the woods. I would have been grateful to never see another tree again, but here we were once again, sleeping out in the open.

We remained in those woods for an additional four more days.

A far cry from the luxurious life of the village.

All four of us slept on the ground, shivering in the cold, predawn light, and throwing ourselves behind the gigantic shadowy trees at the slightest noise.

Things began to get more complicated. These woods, it seemed, were the gathering point for a series of guides, because every day more refugees were joining the party. At least two more came to us every day. Soon we were a group of ten people. Ten people trying to keep out of one another's way, ten people trying their best to keep out of the light. This was when something traumatic occurred to me; something that I have never forgotten. We were the only four children in our party. The others were all adults. At eleven, with Liba and the Landau cousins clocking in at seven, six, and four years old, I was the oldest of the bunch. Not only were we the youngest people there, but we had no one to look after us. It was us against the world.

A woman arrived in the woods with her son. He was a big boy, about sixteen or seventeen years old. Big enough to take care of himself. Not like the young children, little more than babies, I was watching over.

One evening, I was sitting off to the side behind one of the trees when I saw the woman approach the guide and asked to speak with him. I happened to overhear their conversation, and it made my very blood boil. I'm normally a fairly calm person, but this was too much.

"Please," she pleaded. "Please take us first. Get us out of this forest before you take anyone else!"

I couldn't see if the guide was agreeing to her proposition, because a tree was blocking my vision. I could only listen with heightened senses.

"I'll pay you more than we originally agreed upon," she offered. "Just get us out of here!" She was crying and carrying on. I wanted to storm out of my hiding place and slap her right across the face.

I wanted to shout at her, "How dare you! We've been hiding in this forest longer than you, small children with nobody to look after us, no parents to make sure we aren't being taken advantage of. And all you can think about is trying to bribe the guide to get you out first?! Is this the way a Jewish mother behaves?"

I had no money to make a counteroffer. I had nothing. And here was this woman, who not only didn't dream of assisting us, but was trying to take advantage of us! I had grown up in a home where I was surrounded by people like my parents and Zeide Shaya'le. They were *tzaddikim*. They were *chesed* personified. Seeing this kind of selfish, uncaring behavior simply shocked me to the core!

I waited until later, when I saw the guide sitting by himself.

"Can I speak with you for a second?"

"Certainly."

His craggy serious face dissolved into a sudden smile. I couldn't control myself. I burst into tears. I didn't want to do that. I wanted to plead my case like a grown-up, but I wasn't a grown-up, and the tears came pouring out of their own accord.

"Please don't leave us here any longer!" I begged him. "You brought us here first. We've been with you the longest. We've been waiting patiently. But we're so scared in the forest. We don't want to stay here any longer then we absolutely have to. Look at my cousins. They're such small children. They don't deserve this. They need to get out of the forest and into a house with someone to give them food and take care of them. They're just babies. Please have mercy on us and take us out of here in the order that we came."

I saw that he was listening closely. My words were entering his heart.

"I would have been glad to offer you more money," I continued, "but I have nothing. We haven't eaten in days. Who knows better than you how little we have? I'm sorry, but it's the truth. Please don't let money be the reason we get left behind!"

As I pleaded with him, I could tell that he was a sincere man, that he really wanted to save us and bring us to safety, that he was concerned with our making it through the war alive. And I know that he felt terrible about the state we were in. We truly were starving in that forest. Imagine having almost nothing to eat for four complete days!

"Don't worry," he told me in a reassuring voice. "I will never do that to you. You girls deserve to go first, and you will. You've waited a really long time and nobody is going before you."

He was a good man. Even though he was a non-Jew. And that's what made the woman's betrayal so much harder to bear. My mother had sent six children out with the guides before she sent her own. She cared about everyone, not only her own family. Even this gentile was a genuine, honest, and maybe even righteous man.

That woman's actions had rocked my world. She was one of a series of individuals who took away my belief and trust in people and left me, an eleven-year-old, empty in return. And it was all the harder because she was someone whom I'd have expected to do the right thing.

—»·•·«—

Soon enough, we were leaving the shelter of the overgrown trees and moving toward an uncertain future. A carriage pulled up for us and the driver helped us inside, where he proceeded to cover us liberally with straw and sacks of vegetables: potatoes and carrots, cabbage and sweet-smelling corn. He was heading toward a town and the carriage was weighed down by all the produce he was carrying, both to make him money and to use as a smoke screen for the illicit burden concealed underneath.

Our destination was one of Czechoslovakia's major cities. It was a strange feeling to be driving through a big city once again. I hadn't been in such a place since Cracow, and the constant noise sounded foreign to me after the solitude of the forest and mountains. But I was a child of the war and adaptation had become a way of life.

Some days were spent moving from place to place, one house to the next, trying to remain safe and looking fearfully over our shoulders at all times. But the nights were the worst. Tired as I was (and I was constantly exhausted from being on the run), I couldn't allow myself to fall asleep because there was a little six-year-old named Liba who couldn't be trusted at all, and was always threatening to escape back to her mother the moment I turned my back.

Which meant that I could never turn my back.

So Liba slept, and I watched her.

And then morning would arrive, and I would be faced with another full day of survival, of using all my senses and trying to stay sharp—all while operating on virtually no sleep. My eyes were bloodshot and constantly closing against my will. I gritted my teeth and soldiered on.

———»·◦·«———

One night, we stayed at a Jewish home. By this time, my eyes were irritated and horribly red. It took me a while to fall asleep, and when I awoke and tried to open my eyes, I realized that I wasn't able to. They were glued together by tears, pus, and fatigue. I was lying in my bed, trying to figure out what to do, when I heard my hosts mention words that made me prick up my ears and listen closely.

"Why doesn't the Rebbe send his children and *eineklach* over the border as well?"

They were talking about Zeide Shaya'le. My Zeide, whom I loved more than life itself.

I couldn't control myself.

"*Ich bin der Rebbe's a kind*!" I burst out. ("I am a child of the Rebbe!") I was speaking in Yiddish to my grandfather's Chassidim, to people who actually cared about me and my family. It was an incredibly warm feeling, like a homecoming of sorts. The entire time I spoke, I was trying in vain to open my eyes. They refused to open. I was crying, but my eyelids remained glued shut. A strange situation.

The woman of the house helped me. She wet my eyes gently, using a warm washcloth and even strokes, until slowly but surely she cleaned them out and I could finally open them and look around me.

Here were people who actually knew my family, my Mama and Tatte, my uncles and aunts. People who had grown up visiting my grandfather. They were Sanzer Chassidim, and they loved me just because of who I was.

Unconditional love. I informed them that one of my traveling companions was actually my cousin, Miriam Rubin, the granddaughter of the Vizhnitzer Rebbe, which came as a pleasant surprise to them as well. Imagine, they'd been hosting their Rebbe's family without even knowing it. What an honor!

They spoke with us gently. Urged us not to be afraid.

"Don't worry," one of them said to me. "We know exactly where each of you has to go, and we'll make sure that you get there."

I can't describe the relief at knowing that I could finally revert to being a child again. That someone else was going to take charge of my life. That I wouldn't have to make decisions for a while.

They informed each of us where we'd be going next. Soon it was my turn.

"You will be traveling to Bardiyoff, Sima. Your sister is already there, staying at the home of Rav Halberstam, another Gerlitzer grandchild."

It sounded good to me.

CHAPTER TEN

I T WAS LATE 1943, AND I WAS BEGINNING A NEW stage in my life.

I had expected to stay with my sister Devora, but it was decided instead (I don't know by whom) that I would move in with a friend of our family, his two sons, and a nephew. His wife and two daughters had been forced to return to Hungary because she was a Hungarian citizen while her husband was not. This meant that the family was temporarily divided—a not-uncommon phenomenon in those days.

They treated me royally, and I felt right at home. I was able to go outside freely, I had friends to play with, and for the first time in a long while, I could finally relax. I didn't have to worry that someone would start shooting at me like a rabbit, or that I would be sent away to be murdered.

As mentioned, my host's daughters had been forced to leave home with their mother, which meant that there were two available identities for me to assume, whichever one fit me better. I became a member of the Grussgott family, taking the place of their beloved daughter. In the meanwhile, my brothers arrived in town as well, and took up residence at the home of the *shochet.*

Life in Czechoslovakia might have been easier than back home, but it was still life under German rule. One of the Grussgott boys had legal documents that permitted him to have residence there, but the other brother and his cousin were not allowed to be there and were basically living under conditions similar to house arrest. They couldn't go outdoors because they could not risk being seen by some who might report their presence. This made for a somewhat tense atmosphere in the home. Finally, Mr. Grussgott had had enough of the constant fear and decided it was time to move on to Hungary.

"You will come along with me," he said, "posing as my daughter Sarita."

I had been Sarita for a few weeks already and felt that I'd mastered the role pretty well. I could be whoever they wanted me to be. The last few years of my life had been one constant stage performance already.

We left Bardiyoff and traveled to Brataslava, the first stop on the way to Hungary. I traveled with Sarita's papers and everybody was hoping for an uneventful journey. But it was not to be.

Apparently, the Grussgott family had been under scrutiny. Someone must have known that I wasn't his daughter. Someone must have known that one of his sons and his nephew never left the house. And they even knew where and when we were traveling. And whoever this person was, he was not averse to selling this information for the right price.

⸺●⸺

The main train terminal at Brataslava was crowded with travelers. The roar of hundreds of busy people waiting to board a train to their various destinations merged with the beating of our hearts. We were frightened. German soldiers patrolled the terminal, their impassive faces suggesting a complete detachment from everything that was happening around them. But that, we knew, was a misconception. The Nazis knew exactly what was going on. Every time one of them looked at me, I broke into a sweat. Was he going to walk over? Raise his weapon? Scrutinize my papers? Arrest me? Haul me off to jail?

We were living in a crazy world. A world where a person could be thrown into jail just because she hadn't been born an Aryan or a Magyar. I reassured myself by touching Sarita's papers, reminding myself that they were genuine and would protect me in case anything happened. There was nothing to worry about. I was traveling to Hungary with my father. People traveled to Hungary with their fathers all the time. It happened every day. There was no reason for me to worry.

"The train is already here. Are you ready to go?"

I shrugged. I was ready for anything. I had an anxious feeling in my chest. Something was telling me to run again. But where? And how? Should I just abandon Mr. Grussgott in the middle of the Brataslava terminal and go off on my own? I was torn. My sixth sense had always been right before. Maybe I should just run, leave the kindhearted gentleman while I still had the chance?

The train pulled into the terminal. A distant, official-sounding voice announced that boarding would commence in five minutes. All over the terminal people began lining up, papers out to show the soldiers, voices clamoring with questions and stories and raised in laughter as they hoisted their suitcases and valises on their shoulders and prepared to board the train.

The doors opened.

"All aboard!" the conductor called out. Mr. Grussgott motioned to me, "Let's go."

I trusted him. He was treating me like his very own daughter; he was close to my family and he knew my Zeide. Without him, I had no idea what to do next. And yet, I had a feeling inside that told me something was going to go wrong very soon. Still, what was my alternative? There was none.

So I boarded the train with him, and we found our seats. We tried to remain as inconspicuous as possible, but it wasn't long before we heard them drawing near. The Germans.

They were coming to check our papers.

"Don't worry. Act cheerful and confident. We can pull this off."

My "father" spoke with assurance, but I wasn't so sure. I'd been caught in a train station before. Was it going to happen again? The soldiers were going from seat to seat. They studied every set of documents with eagle eyes. This was no game.

They reached our row.

"Papers, *bitte*." A young soldier was holding out his hand, requesting—no, ordering—us to hand over our papers for inspection. Mr. Grussgott handed his to the soldier. I did the same. The Nazi trooper was just a boy. The same age as my brother Chaim. A child, really. Would he know that Sarita was already living in Hungary, and that I was trying to pull a fast one over their heads?

His eyes went from the papers back to me. The papers to me. Back and forth.

"Stand up," he said his eyes going completely blank. There was no feeling in those eyes. "These documents aren't valid."

He turned to Mr. Grussgott. "Are you this girl's father?"

He could have said no. I would have understood. But,

as I said, during the war some people slipped out of their responsibilities and cared only about themselves, while others stood up to the realities of our life and were ready to sacrifice themselves for others. To his eternal credit, Mr. Grussgott accepted responsibility for the situation.

"Yes, I am." He said it gracefully, although why should he have had to do this? I wasn't even related to him. He was a truly incredible man.

He stood up.

So did I.

Everyone in our carriage pretended to be totally absorbed in the book they were reading or in the breathtaking scenery flashing past us outside the window. No one was willing to spare us as much as a glance. That could be dangerous. If they felt any sympathy, they kept it well hidden.

When the train rolled to a stop at the next station, the soldiers escorted us off. It was hard to believe. One second, I'd been a free person. The next, I was a prisoner again.

<hr/>

The soldiers escorted us from the train. You'd think that a person would lose any semblance of embarrassment after a while, but I was still mortified to see all the other passengers staring openly at me. Some grinned, others kept their expressions carefully neutral; in a very few I could detect a trace of sympathy. We were marched down the platform, past numerous trains headed to points all over Europe, past benches full of gentiles who laughed and made catcalls. We were marched out of the station, and out of their lives. They wouldn't have to think about the prisoners they'd just seen. They could allow the sight to become a fleeting memory.

But we didn't have that luxury. We were going to jail.

The prison was exceedingly large, or perhaps that's just

the way it seemed to a child. It was built in a square shape, with cells all around the outer and inner walls of the building and a giant courtyard in the center. Privacy was a dream of the past. The lights were always on and the guards felt no compunction whatsoever about paying the inmates a visit whenever the fancy struck them.

That first day, after spending some time in our cell, we were led into an empty office on one side of the compound. I saw a closet with cleaning supplies. A desk and chair. Paper, pens, ordinary office supplies. A bookcase filled with books. Everything looked banal and ordinary, except for the little girl and Mr. Grussgott.

There were at least two soldiers present during the course of a normal interrogation.

Two boyishly good-looking officers to take turns, so that one of them would be able to carry on with the job when the other grew weary.

Grussgott was standing against the wall when it began. The look on his face was like steel—as if he was going to hold out no matter what they did to him. Inside, I was crying .

He wasn't my father, or even a relative. Why was he the one who had been chosen to undergo torture for me?

"Who is this girl?" Officer one.

"My daughter, Sarita Grussgott."

"Tell me the truth! Who is she?"

"My daughter Sarita."

"The truth, you Jewish pig!"

"I am telling you the truth!"

"No, you're not." The yell was accompanied by a smack from the Nazi's baton.

"I'm telling the truth! She's my daughter! Sarita."

"Are you his daughter?" Question directed at me.

"Yes, yes! Stop hitting him!"

"We're going to stop hitting him when he tells us the truth."

"What makes you think I'm not telling you the truth?"

"We know all about you. Everything. We have inside information. She doesn't even resemble Sarita." Slap. Slap.

"Ow. Stop hitting me. I promise you this is my daughter. I don't know where you're getting your information from, but it's not correct. This is my daughter, and I'm her father!"

Both of them began beating him now, together and separately. He held his hands up over his head in an effort to protect himself, but the blows rained mercilessly down on his weakened body while I watched in horror. Finally, I shut my eyes so I wouldn't have to see this kind man being beaten to a pulp. Why didn't he just admit the truth? I would understand.

"Tell us the truth! Who is she?"

"I *am* telling you the truth." Slam. Slam.

Finally I couldn't bear it any longer. I got up off the chair and ran over to the soldier who was hitting him. I grabbed his arm and yelled, "Stop hitting my father! Can't you see you hurt him enough? Leave him alone!"

The officer looked down at me with a shocked expression on his face, as if he couldn't even fathom that a dirty, disgusting Jew girl would dare sully his sleeve with her contaminated hand. He shoved me away, sending me flying across the office and into a file cabinet.

But my interruption had broken their momentum. They glanced at each other, as if uncertain what they should do next.

I wasn't surprised when they elected to take a brief coffee break. When they returned, it had been decided that an interrogation was no place for a child of my tender years. (Especially one brave enough to attack the interrogators.) And so, I was removed to the cell that I shared with Mr.

Grussgott—while he was forced to remain with his interrogators and undergo additional torture, because they were still convinced that he was lying.

This happened day after day.

Have you any idea what it feels like to know that a man who cares about you, your protector, a person willing to lay his life on the line for you, is undergoing torture every day—because of you? Do you know how absolutely horrific a thought that is? Talk about guilt!

"I'm so sorry," I'd sob to him when he returned to the cell. But he just smiled at me and acted as if everything was fine. I could hear his screams from down the corridor. The beating and the shouting and the sound of someone struck so hard he can't catch his breath. And when he regains it, the pain is so bad that he just wants to die so it will be over.

So it went, day after day. They kept removing Mr. Grussgott from our cell, yelling at him, interrogating him and trying to force him to admit the truth. It wasn't working. And so, one fine day, they brought me along for the ride.

"Tell us the truth, little girl," one of the officers yelled at me, his handsome face tense with anger. "This man isn't really your father!"

"YES, HE IS MY FATHER!" I yelled back at him. "He is, he is!"

This went on for the next few days. Then, one day, they removed Mr. Grussgott from the interrogation room for a short while, leaving me behind.

"Don't do anything or go anywhere," they ordered me.

I sat there innocently, shrugging my shoulders as if to say, *Where could I go, anyway?*

The second they were out of the room, I went to work. I stood up and made my way to one of the windows, which I opened a little bit. Then I went over to the next window and opened that one a smidgen. I moved between the two of them so it wouldn't look too suspicious if someone happened to walk into the room while I was toying with the windows. The longer they stayed out of the room, and the more time I had to myself, the more those windows were opened.

A stiff breeze entered the office. Before I knew it, papers were flying every which way, documents that had been left on the desk soaring in the biting wind that filled every corner of the room.

What was the interrogator going to accuse me of? Opening the window? I wanted some air.

He was so angry when he reentered the room and saw the mess that the wind had made of it. He'd left it tidy, but there wasn't a paper in its proper place by the time he returned.

But he knew me well enough by now to realize that a scolding would be futile. Although I was scared out of my wits by the interrogators, I never failed to yell at them whenever I had the chance. As they took turns hitting Mr. Grussgott with their wooden batons, I'd stand there screaming at them with as much force as my high-pitched voice could command: "Don't you hit my father! Don't you hit my father!"

Being yelled at like that takes a lot of the enjoyment out of beating someone.

"My father! Tatte! Tatte! Stop beating him"

When they asked me questions, I never stopped defending Mr. Grussgott or vociferously claiming that he was my father and that they were making a big mistake. Shockingly enough, they did not hit me. To this day, I can't figure out why they didn't do something to silence me.

It was a horrible time in my life—though nothing compared to what my "father" was going through. There was a tiny window high up in my cell, and if I stood on the sloping cement and stretched on my tippytoes, I could just manage to see outside. But there was never anything to see.

The prison was an endless concrete maze that made the prisons of Israel and the United States nowadays seem like country clubs in comparison. We slept on concrete, and it was cold. Always cold. And the dreams that came to us as we slept made an already terrible experience even worse. I dreamed of people chasing me, in hot pursuit forever, while I kept on running, running, running for my life. I dreamed of Nazi soldiers coming to get me, and dogs barking —

Eventually, the interrogators lost patience with us. Someone higher up decided that we should be moved. Listening to the talk between the guards, it sounded as though we were going to be escorted to Budapest.

In Hungary.

Hungary. That had been our original destination. Perhaps we hadn't envisioned ourselves entering the grand city of Budapest under armed escort, but it would bring us many steps closer to our goal. Also, it was wonderful to get out of that concrete jail, where it was always cold and Mr. Grussgott was always being beaten.

Maybe things would change for the better in the land of goulash, waltzes, and the beautiful "Blue Danube."

HUNGARY

CHAPTER ELEVEN

T HE POLICE WOKE US VERY EARLY IN THE MORNing, and we were roughly informed that we had ten minutes to get our things together before we departed.

"Where are you taking us?" Mr. Grussgott wanted to know.

"You'll find out everything in good time, stinking Jew."

Soon enough, we were leaving the cement prison. A vehicle pulled up outside the prison doors and we were motioned inside. Moments later, we had pulled away from the curb and were heading for the nearest train station. Destination: Budapest. It seemed they were merely transferring us from one prison to another. Maybe they hoped that the authorities in Budapest would be able to ferret out the truth from us.

We were accompanied at all times by an officer of the law, meant to ensure that nobody escaped.

The terminal was busy at this time of day. People were coming and going to and from all points of the country. We took seats at the edge of the platform to wait for the next train. Kiosks opened for business. Some sold coffee and drinks, others offered food. They were doing a brisk trade.

Steam from pans full of "*letcho*" wafted from all directions. There was another stand where a man fried "bundash" for anyone who cared to eat his breakfast on the run. The appetizing aromas came at me from every direction. They merged in my stomach and made me feel sick. The smoke from the ever-present cigarettes, the scent of freshly percolating coffee, the nauseating smells of the *tereifeh* food that was being prepared on the spot. It made me feel sick to think that I could find *tereifeh* food even the slightest bit appealing.

Before long, the train arrived. The policeman ordered us to board. He found us seats in the center of the carriage. We sat in a row: Mr. Grussgott, the policeman, and then me. Porters rushed here and there, loading the train. Crying children boarded with their mothers and were shushed and plied with food to keep them content. I could hear the conductor's calls resounding through the station, and the toot-toot of the whistle as the train slowly picked up speed. Soon we had left the station behind and the sootiness of the city gave way to open fields and tall forests.

The feeling of unease in my stomach didn't let up. In fact, it grew worse. I could feel the bile rising in my throat, was afraid I was going to throw up all over the train. Frantically, I got the policeman's attention by motioning at my throat and stomach—pantomiming how I was going to be sick.

Either he didn't believe me, or he didn't care. He disregarded my signals and motioned for me to stay right where I was. So it was his own fault when I threw up seconds later— all over his sleeve!

I must have been extremely ill, because it didn't even stop then. I really couldn't control myself. I was like a faucet of horrible, disgusting water that wouldn't turn off, no matter how hard I tried.

The officer's face went through a series of rapid color changes. He turned red with utter embarrassment and then purple with anger. He was furious. So furious that he could barely speak. Finally, he opened his mouth.

"How *dare* you do such a thing, you stupid Jew-girl?" he roared, his spit flying in every direction. "How dare you throw up on me! Now I smell, and the whole carriage smells! What on earth is wrong with you?!"

I would have apologized, but another jolt of the carriage sent me into a spasm which ended in another bout of vomiting, landing once again right on his uniform! He was so angry that he was literally frothing at the mouth. That soldier was completely at a loss. He'd been peacefully doing his job, sitting on the train and guarding his two prisoners, his uniform and boots immaculate as ever. And the next thing he knew, this terrible Jewish brat had vomited all over him. Everything smelled: the train, the floor, and best of all, the officer.

Mr. Grussgott was chagrined, though he couldn't suppress his laughter.

"What have you done?" he asked me in laughing desperation. His smile was tinged with fear. Who knew what the policeman would do to us now?

We waited fearfully for the officer's reaction which, strangely enough, did not arrive. Maybe he knew that he had only himself to blame. If he would have let me leave the carriage in time, none of this would have happened.

<hr />

The train pulled into the station. We had arrived. Budapest at last.

Beautiful, gracious Budapest, city of culture, music, and gaiety; a city where the broad boulevards and public squares were lined with art.

Budapest. The cosmopolitan capitol of Hungary.

Goulash. Letcho. Chicken Paprikash. Dancing to the "Blue Danube." Waltzes and culture. Delicious food and beautiful hotels. The wonderful Danube River that separated the Buda section of the city from the Pest section, with its graceful bridges and parks on the riverbank. This was the world of the Magyar, with his fancy downtown homes and exclusive stores. Stone edifices carved with immaculate designs. Jews had always been a part of this world, but now it seemed their destiny had managed to catch up with them.

Hungary's official leader was named Horthy—a man vigorously opposed to a Nazi takeover of his country. And yet the Hungarians possessed their very own branch of fascist leadership, which sponsored the Arrow Cross, a vicious group of thugs and armed robbers very much akin to the German SS. The Hungarian Magyars hated their Jewish countrymen and compatriots. It made no difference to them that the Jews had been part of Hungary's history for hundreds of years. By and large, they were almost as passionate about hating the children of Avraham as the Germans themselves.

A fine mix, the city of Budapest. A future killing ground.

Our faithful escort, who I'm sure by now wanted nothing more to do with either one of us ever again, delivered us to the largest jail in Budapest. This type of jail was home to criminals and murderers, sentenced to life behind massive walls and curled, barbed-wire fences. It was no place for a young girl. Yet this was to be my new residence.

A large percentage of the prisoners here were Gypsies who made no attempt to blend in with the rest of the prison population. And it wasn't only the convicts who resided in this facility. Their extended families, young and old, were inside as well, all living together behind bars because their fathers were killers. These Gypsies were extremely dangerous, with no respect or regard for another's life.

The vast majority of the prison's inhabitants were there because either they, or a member of their family, had committed a crime such as theft or murder. But I had been interred for political reasons, the only child in the jail that fit into this category. That was why the powers who ran the prison allowed me to wander freely through the corridors of the most dangerous prison in the country. I was allowed free access through the labyrinth of cells, given the right to walk wherever my feet took me, and to stare at whomever I wished with blatant curiosity. My "father," on the other hand, was forced to remain in our cell from morning till night, unless they were interrogating him.

The prison was a paradox.

Hardened murderers and their apple-cheeked children, some of whom had not yet learned how to speak, sitting side by side behind bars as though it were the most natural thing in the world. With so many children in the prison, they couldn't be completely ignored. A Catholic priest surfaced from time to time to take the children out of their cells and bring them for a supervised visit to the prison's courtyard, where the guards kept a sharp eye on their charges from the beginning to the end of their time together.

I was invited to join these little outings, and I accepted the invitation with grateful relief. Feeling real sunlight on my face was so nice, and so unexpected, that it was worth having to endure Gypsy company to enjoy it. Who would have ever imagined that the great-granddaughter of the Divrei Chaim of Sanz would romp alongside Gypsy children in the most vaunted and fearsome jail in all of Hungary! But beggars can't be choosers, and if that was the only time they allowed me out into the yard, I would take what I was offered.

So I went outside and I played. But I was an adult pretending to be a child, worrying the entire time whether we'd be able to get out of prison or if we were going to be stuck in this infernal place forever.

One afternoon, while out in the yard, I found a stick lying on the courtyard ground and took possession of it. I hadn't had a toy in ages. I was getting a little old for toys, but this stick called out to me, and not wanting to completely relinquish my childhood I began carrying it with me wherever I went. I guess you could call it my lifeline to normalcy.

—————

Although it felt as if we'd been abandoned by the world, that wasn't exactly true. The network of devoted *Yidden* who were aware of everything that was going on in the prisons of Eastern Europe knew about us as well, and were negotiating for our release on a daily basis. They offered money—even a lot of money—but the officers were fairly sure of our guilt and thought they had us nailed. That being the case, they were in no rush to let us go, money or no money.

Meanwhile, it seemed to us that we'd been forgotten by the entire world, that nobody missed us or cared that we had been interred in Hungary's most infamous prison.

—————

I never found out exactly when Mr. Grussgott's wife passed away, but I do know that he learned about it while we were together in prison. She had been sick for a while, and I think her illness was one of the reasons he'd been so keen to get to Budapest. But he never managed to say goodbye.

Meanwhile, the police hadn't given up hope of incriminating us and they consistently continued to interrogate my "father." He was called out of his cell and taken for questioning almost every day. Many a lesser person would have cracked long before, but Mr. Grussgott just held on and never let them get to him, no matter what they did. And it must have hurt him. A lot.

After his wife died, they began trying a new tactic.

"Let's say we believe your story that this is little Sarita," his interrogator said cunningly. "Let's say we're coming around to your story. I still have a question for you."

"My father" waited warily for the next attack on his credibility.

"If she is your daughter, then why doesn't she care that her mother passed away?"

"What do you mean?"

"What do I mean? I mean that a normal child becomes sad, pensive, withdrawn, and distraught when her mother passes away. That's a fact of life. Yet your 'daughter' seems not to have been affected even in the slightest way. She acts exactly as she did before your wife died. Doesn't that make you wonder? It certainly makes *me* wonder!"

Mr. Grussgott looked them in the eye.

"You're making a really good point. Very convincing."

They waited to see where he would go from here.

"Except for one thing."

"And that is?"

"And that is the fact that I haven't told her about her mother's passing."

"You haven't told your daughter that her mother passed away? What's wrong with you?"

"What good can it do for her to know this while in prison? Do you really think this is the right place to inform her that she will never see her mother again? The news would only serve to depress her, and that's the last thing I want to accomplish!"

He spoke with such confidence. The policemen exchanged glances. They hadn't thought of that one. It was a testimony to Mr. Grussgott's brilliance and ingenuity, a trait he'd come to polish and perfect all because of me. In the end, they accepted his story and allowed him to return to our cell.

———⬩◦⬩———

One day, after being let out of my cell, I began walking through the corridor between the cells, banging my stick on every fifth tile or so (a game I originated while in jail), when I happened to glance into one of the nearby cells and saw someone sitting there. I'd already walked past the cell when I did a double take and reversed my steps to take a good look at him again—because I'd recognized the person inside.

It was someone I had known back in the Bochnia ghetto.

Not only had I known him, but he'd been one of the leaders of the Judenrat. A man of power.

Later, he would tell me how he'd developed a relationship with a certain Nazi officer while in his position as Judenrat head. Enough of a relationship that the Nazi pulled him over one day.

"Rapps?"

"Yes, sir?"

"I could get in trouble for telling you this, but I want you to know that you won't be needed here for much longer. Escape now, while you still can."

That was why he'd run away. And now he had been captured, and was sitting in jail.

I may have been young, but I knew that this was not a good development. What if he recognized me, and inadvertently told the authorities that I was not related to Mr. Grussgott? The thought filled me with fear. I didn't know what to do.

I later learned that Rapps was afraid, too. He was using

the alias of a Polish gentile and was terrified that I, who had doubtless recognized him, would give his secret away. I knew that I had to let him know right away what name I was currently using. That way, we would both be able to look out for each other.

I couldn't just sidle over to his cell; that would have raised too many questions. But I could play with my stick. I could throw it up in the air and catch it and drop it by mistake and watch it roll toward his cell. And when I ran after it to try and stop it, I could straighten up in front of him for a second and say through clenched teeth, "My name is Sarita Grussgott and I'm from Czechoslovakia."

He nodded to show that he understood the importance of what I was telling him. Then he gave me his Polish name, so I would know what to say in case anyone troubled to ask.

Now that I knew there was someone else in the jail from Bochnia, I was filled with intense curiosity. I was sure that Rapps knew what had happened to my parents, to my brothers and sisters, and Zeide Shaya'le. I wanted to know the truth. It was so hard to lie awake at night wondering about everyone I loved so much. Of course, I knew that the chances of their still being alive were very slim; I might have been young but I was far from stupid. I knew firsthand what the Germans were all about. Still, one can always hope. Without hope, what do we have?

Part of me whispered fiercely, savagely, that I shouldn't try to find out.

What if they are no longer alive? How will you deal with that?

But another part of me silenced the first part. I needed to face whatever the reality was. I had a right to find out if my family was still alive, and I intended to do so.

Morning dawned. I could see the sky gradually turning the palest pink, and then the pink merged with burnt orange and a tinge of red. And then everything was rosy because the sun had risen and the world was glowing with the vitality of a new day. I banged on my cell door for a guard as soon as I was able.

A guard appeared, like a well-trained robot, to let me out of my cell. He opened the cell door.

I had managed to learn a few words of Hungarian in the short period of time that I'd spent as a guest of the Hungarian government.

"Thank you, Lazlo."

"You're very welcome, young lady."

The guards liked me because they thought I was cute and I made them laugh. Maybe I reminded them of their little girls at home, safe and sound in the kitchen with their mothers. Seconds later, I was out of my cell and walking jauntily in the direction of my new friend.

How wonderful that I didn't have to pretend with Mr. Rapps. I didn't have to answer to the name "Sarita Grussgott." I didn't have to be someone that I wasn't. Have you any idea what a relief that was? I could finally be myself again. I pranced along the hallway with my stick, the very picture of childish exuberance. I was going to meet my source, my fountain of information.

I pretended to be playing a game — a game that led me directly to the cell where he sat waiting for me, probably dreading my return. He'd known that I would come back. He didn't want to tell me what I wanted to know, but everyone has a right to the truth. Mr. Rapps sat alone, his eyes full of the anguish particular to people who sit in a jail cell for hours at a time, days at a time, with nothing to look forward to. People who long to be free, but fear that they will never be free again.

"Please tell me what happened to my family," I whispered.

"If we survive this war," he said slowly, looking up at me, "don't go searching for your family. Your parents are no longer alive." (The pain was like white-hot needles piercing me in every direction.)

"Zeide Shaya'le is no longer among the living either." (This was somehow even more scorching.)

Every word he said was worse than the one preceding it.

"Chaim may have survived, because they sent him to Auschwitz. Maybe he'll be one of the lucky ones to make it through that door to Hell."

Somehow, I found my voice. "But what happened to them?"

"Your mother was hiding in a bunker. Every day, someone took a turn leaving the bunker to go out in search of bread. One day it was your mother's turn. But the Germans caught her and shot her as she searched for bread."

I shuddered. Mama gone. It was almost impossible to conceive of such a thing.

The look he gave me was one of infinite pity.

"The Germans dug three mass graves near the Bochnia ghetto."

I turned white. Mass graves. My holy father, buried in a mass grave! Zeide Shaya'le, flung into a mass grave... Modest, dignified Mama... I was sure she had remained that way until her final moment.

"The Germans herded together the remainder of the ghetto, the last few who had somehow survived the years of German *aktions*, who had managed to hide and outfox the enemy. They were taken at gunpoint to the edge of the graves, and shot.

"That was how they died."

The world turned black in front of my eyes. Tears filled them, so that I could hardly see the man talking to me.

"I was there at the end," he whispered. "Right before I managed to escape. I saw your father and your Zeide during those final moments."

I looked at him, consumed with jealousy. He had been there at the end! How I envied him!

"I even spoke to your Zeide," he added.

"Your spoke to Zeide Shaya'le?"

"Yes, Sima."

"What did you talk about?" The tears were pouring from my eyes now.

"He had a request for me."

"A request? What kind of request?"

"He wanted me to make sure that he was buried in a *tallis*."

"Were you able to carry out his request?"

His eyes were full of tears, too. He shook his head in the negative.

"How could I? The area was full of Nazi soldiers. I don't even know how I managed to escape alive. It was a sheer miracle, every step of the way. I would have given anything to be able to bury your Zeide, Sima. But there was no way."

There was a moment of silence, and then Mr. Rapps continued his story.

"'Reb Shaya'le,' I said to him, 'please give me your shoe.'"

"What did you want Zeide's shoe for?"

"If I couldn't bury him, at least I could bury his shoe. The holy shoe that adorned his holy foot."

"And you buried his shoe? That you managed to do?"

He nodded. "That was one of the last things I did before leaving Bochnia forever."

It was at the moment that I knew that nothing would ever be the same again. My world had changed in an irrevocable way. I was filled with a terrible, gut-wrenching anguish that made me want to rip my hair out and bang my head against the wall. I wanted to die.

I returned to my cell, where I sat down in the corner of the room, a low sound emerging from my mouth that seemed to go on and on without a beginning or an end. And then I started to cry again.

I hadn't cried like this since the beginning of the war. I wept and screamed and thrashed around the floor, reverting back to babyhood, not caring if the policemen wondered why on earth I had suddenly gone insane. In fact, the officers did come into the room, wanting to know what had transpired to turn the normally cheerful Sima into this wild-eyed child who was rolling around the floor and screaming as if the very world had come to an end.

And Mr. Grussgott, dear Mr. Grussgott, turned to the officers and said, "I couldn't keep it from her anymore. I had to tell her about her mother. You wanted to know why she wasn't crying. Well, now she is. I hope you're satisfied."

They turned and left.

If those men harbored any more suspicions about us, they were dashed there and then, as I lay on the floor and screamed my hurt and pain into the cold cement. Now that they knew it was my mother who had died, all their doubts disappeared. And, ironically, it was true. I *had* just learned that my mother had died. My tears were genuine. There was nothing fake about the way I was acting, and I guess the officers were finally convinced.

Those tears, along with a good dose of bribery, helped to finally wrap things up.

The two-pronged ticket to our release from prison: money and the death of my mother.

Because somebody had to die.

CHAPTER TWELVE

WALKING OUT OF THE BUDAPEST JAIL INTO the open air of a normal street was cause for glorious rejoicing. To have been locked up in a prison for five endless months, and to suddenly have been released, for no other reason than the fact that I had shown true and uncomplicated emotion, defied belief. We were free!

I glanced over at Mr. Grussgott and laughed in pure exultation. Budapest was breathtaking that morning. Every leaf a different color. Every color made up of twenty shades. Every shade more vibrant than I remembered. I felt so alive! I could hear the world singing along with my heart.

WE WERE FREE! You can't imagine what freedom is if you've never experienced its opposite, as we had. And now it was over. We left the forbidding walls of the prison—just walked out between the giant metal gates and listened to them clang shut behind us. I looked back for a second at the guard towers and steel bars and the narrow windows which allowed tiny bits of light into every cell, and I breathed deeply of the intoxicating air of freedom.

A mother passed by, pushing a baby carriage.

Two schoolgirls skipped past, laughing and arguing over something that was large to them and inconceivably small to me.

A trolley car came to a sudden halt, sparks shooting out from beneath its metal wheels. People boarded, paid the driver, and took their seats. We boarded as well; it was time to move on.

Goodbye, jail. I'll never forget the time I spent with you. I would like to, but I know I never will.

Just behind and adjacent to the glorious Budapest Opera House is a street with the unlikely name of O Ut.

212 O Ut. This was in the Pest section of the capital, the exclusive part of the city. The river Danube served as the unofficial barrier between Buda (where the poor and average citizens lived) and Pest, where old money and genteel breeding lunched at pricey restaurants with foreign names, and diplomats wrote letters to their families back home extolling the exquisite manners and delicious burgundy wine of the Hungarian upper class.

212 O Ut was the home of Rav Baruch Rabinovitch, esteemed Munkatcher Rebbe and a second or third cousin of mine through the Yehudi Hakadosh. This was where we headed upon our release from prison. The present-day Munkatcher Rebbe is one of Rav Baruch's youngest sons; I remember carrying him around and playing with him whenever I had a chance.

The Rabinovitch home was a wonderful place to be in after everything I'd been through. I'd been forced to survive on nothing but a few tiny pears for days on end while hiking through miles of forests and swimming across treacherous rivers. I'd been forced to plead with a taciturn peasant not to leave me behind in the middle of nowhere. I'd endured long months of prison life. And now, here I was, sitting once again at a Shabbos table with a lace tablecloth and crystal utensils.

Oh, to be human again! To smell the aroma of chicken soup with *lukshen*. To see people smiling with natural ease and warmth. To hear words of Torah from the mouth of a man whom my Zeide would have felt comfortable being around.

That's the world. One moment a person is being chased like an animal, and the next he is sitting perfectly comfortable at the sweetest Shabbos table in the world, and sleeping on the softest Hungarian linen imaginable.

Although I wanted nothing more than to relax and recover at my cousin's home, Mr. Grussgott had other plans for me.

"I want you to go visit the Belzer Rebbe."

"I don't want to visit anyone."

"I know, but I would really appreciate it if you at least paid your respects to one of the leading rebbes of Europe. You know that Reb Shaya'le would have wanted you to do this."

That was true. And using *Der Zeide's* name was also the best way to reach my heart. Had Zeide Shaya'le been in Budapest, he would probably have gone to visit the Belzer Rebbe himself. He wasn't here, but I was. It was up to me. Mr. Grussgott accompanied me to the Rebbe's house, making sure that I didn't get lost on the way.

There were long lines of people waiting to see the Belzer Rebbe. When I arrived at the house and presented myself, I was taken inside immediately and given an audience with the Rebbe a short time later. My "father" waited with the multitudes, while I was shown into the inner sanctum.

The Rebbe, who was very elderly at the time, was sitting at the head of the table. He did not look at me, but he did ask me a number of questions. Then he offered me some money. All in all, the meeting was over almost before it even began.

⸺⸱⸱⸱⸺

Rav Baruch's home was a happy one. There were four young boys constantly getting into mischief, and I knew I could teach them a thing or two if I put my mind to it. Unfortunately, I wasn't as young as I had once been. It was as if a grown-up had invaded my body and replaced my soul with that of someone fifteen years my senior. It didn't take me long to realize that my cousin, the Munkatcher Rebbe—idyllic as his life may have seemed—was a man torn by contradictory desires.

Part of him wanted to flee. That part chafed at the knowledge of what was taking place on the killing grounds of Eastern Europe. It commanded him to leave—to escape Hungary and run away to Eretz Yisrael. But the more conservative part of him, the part that was used to listening to his parents, wouldn't allow him to obey that inner voice, because his mother-in-law refused to even hear of leaving.

"What for?" she asked.

And she could even be forgiven for asking that question.

There were no Germans in Hungary at that time, and no prospect of their coming. They would only arrive on March 19, 1944. But she wasn't a seer. She couldn't foretell the future. Right now, it was safer in neutral Hungary than in the uncivilized wilds of British-ruled Palestine, and *derech eretz* wouldn't even allow him to contemplate the idea. And even though his mother-in-law lived in Munkatch and the

Rebbe and his family lived right beside the opera house in Budapest, she still held tremendous sway over the family.

But Rav Baruch was like me. He wanted to run. The Rebbe might have been young in years and life experience—perhaps only in his late thirties—but his heart knew that he needed to leave. And yet, he couldn't.

And that was why the Munkatcher Rebbe was filled with an unbearable sadness that would not go away. His *neshamah* sensed the madness that was approaching, and was constantly urging him to get moving before it was too late.

<hr style="width:20%">

My little brothers, Usher and Chaskel Duvid, had been smuggled over the border from Czechoslovakia as well. They were the youngest of the group, struggling to keep up with the older children and their guide. Eventually they crossed the turbulent river/border and were successful in reaching Hungary.

This would have been cause for celebration—were it not for the fact that they were caught by the Hungarian police in Kashau, and escorted to the very prison in which I had been a guest just a short time before.

Even now, as I remember, my heart goes out to them. Two little boys, all alone in a gigantic prison surrounded by Gypsies and hardened murderers, playing in their cell and waiting for the day when someone would come and call their name.

And then, one day, it happened.

Necessity as we all know, is the mother of invention. Jews by nature are not spies or espionage agents. But there comes a time in a person's life when he is in danger, and the only way to save himself is by steadily and accurately acquiring the knowledge that his enemy possesses. And that was why an entire network was put into operation. A network that provided false papers for those looking to flee hostile countries or to evade the police. *Yidden* who made sure to use every contact they had, to uncover every bit of information that existed.

Who had been arrested?

Why? What could be done to get him out?

Was his family taken care of?

And so on —

Once they had the necessary information, the network had to decide on the best way to go about dealing with the situation.

Should they bribe the gentiles?

And, if so, how much?

There were so many variables involved. What worked for Germans didn't work for Poles, and vice versa. But the ancient adage definitely did apply: Every man has his price. And it was the network's job to figure out what that was.

As soon as they heard that Rav Shaya'le's two grandsons were being held in that infamous, rat-infested hellhole, they sprang into action. It wasn't long before they had managed to secure the boys' release from Hungary's worst prison and had them transferred to a minimum-security jail where no murderers or Gypsies were housed and where visitors were allowed on a daily basis.

I was informed by a network member that it was now possible to visit my brothers. You can imagine how happy—no, how overjoyed—I felt.

Usher. Chaskel Duvid. My baby brothers.

Although it hadn't been that long since we'd been split up in the Bochnia ghetto, it seemed like an eternity. So much had happened since those terrible days.

We were now orphans. Our parents were gone. Removed to a better world. Zeide Shaya'le had been taken from us, too. We were almost completely alone in the world. There was no question in my mind that I would visit my brothers as soon as I had recovered from my ordeal of the last few months.

I didn't ask Rav Baruch Rabinovitch for permission. Visiting a jail, any jail, would have made him too anxious. He would have felt that it was forbidden to place oneself in the lion's den. But by then I was long past the stage where I felt the need to ask anyone's permission before I made a move. Those days were gone.

For better or for worse, I made my own decisions now.

———»·◦·«———

I was never one for staying home and doing nothing. As soon as my recuperation from my ordeal had come to an end, I made plans to see my brothers. But first, I wanted to find out a little more about the place I was in. Part of this came from a natural urge to get to know the neighborhood around me, but there was an added factor that prompted me to leave the house and become acquainted with my surroundings. My gut was sending me warning signals.

True, the Germans weren't here yet. But that didn't mean they weren't going to come. That's what we had foolishly believed in Poland—and look how wrong we'd been.

This time, I was determined to be prepared. Just in case.

And that meant getting to know the lay of the land.

———»·◦·«———

The Munkatcher Rebbe's home was situated right behind the Opera House, a locale well suited for such a highly esteemed personage. You couldn't ask for a more prestigious address in Budapest. I stepped through the door and began walking down gracious, tree-lined streets dotted with luxurious mansions.

I saw chauffeurs in livery helping children in school uniforms into expensive cars. As I strolled along the pristine sidewalks, I looked down at my new boots, new coat, and new gloves, all benevolent gifts of the Satmar Rebbetzin. She had come to visit a few days earlier, loaded down with presents. I hadn't had a new article of clothing since — I couldn't remember when. And here I was, the proud owner of a delightfully warm and fluffy coat, woolen gloves that kept my hands toasty warm, and boots that would have been the pride and joy of any girl back in Sucha—or Cracow, for that matter.

The Satmar Rebbetzin had really superb taste.

But what was even better than the feel of all this new clothing was the warm feeling in my heart that came along with the gifts.

Someone cared about me.

Enough to visit me. Enough to splurge on such splendid gifts.

It made me want to sing!

The trolley pulled up at my stop and I boarded with pride, knowing how good I looked. I fit right into this exclusive neighborhood. What a far cry I was from where I had been just a short while before, huddled beneath a tree, shivering from the intense cold in the middle of an endless forest — or incarcerated in a cold, hostile prison.

Not anymore. Now I had a home.

———⧓⧓———

The trolley took me through the city, past expensive hotels and beautiful buildings, alongside parks full of green where children frolicked and pets ran in the sunshine. I rode on until I reached another kind of building: the jail where my brothers were being held captive.

I exited the trolley by the prison. Although I knew that

this was a minimum-level facility and nothing like the one I'd spent so much time in, my heart began beating much more quickly. My hands were clammy and my pulse was racing. Logic had nothing to do with my body's reaction. I looked up at the prison gates, and I was reduced to senseless terror.

The guards at the entrance allowed me in without any questions. Not only did they let me in, they even escorted me to my brothers' cell. And there they were: Usher and Chaskel Duvid. As cute as ever. Corkscrew *peyos* bobbing as they moved, their shy faces alight with the pleasure of our reunion. We talked for a long time. I wanted to know every detail of what they had gone through. But they could barely remember.

"Did you stay in the forest for a long time?"

They exchanged glances and shrugged. "We don't remember."

"Was the gentile nice to you?"

"Yes."

"Were you afraid?"

"Yes."

"Were you hungry?"

This, they recalled. "All the time."

"You poor boys. And how is it now?"

"A little better than before. But we're still cold. All the time."

"I'm sure you are." Looking around at the stone walls of the drafty prison, I shuddered at the thought of being locked up in a place like this again. But here were my brothers, shaking with cold during the long nights, acting brave, and trying not to cry.

I reached down and I pulled off first one beautiful glove, and then the other. The gifts from the Satmar Rebbetzin. Gifts that obviously were not meant for me.

"Usher," I said, "Chaskel Duvid. Do you see these gloves?"

They nodded.

"I want you to have them. They're for you."

They were too young to even protest that they couldn't accept them. No, they took them, and rejoiced in their good fortune. Later on they would tell me that they took turns wearing my gloves during the long, freezing nights. Each of them would put on the deliciously warm gloves for a few minutes, or sometimes they each wore one glove. They were trying to keep warm, trying to survive: the lot of Jewish children in those dark days.

———❖———

Knowing that my seven- and eight-year-old brothers were languishing in prison left me with no peace of mind. The problem was, there was nothing I could do about it. I was a person who tried to take action whenever possible, but in this case I felt utterly helpless.

And then, one day, I was visiting an old friend from Poland and saw the motorcycle.

A tiny toy motorcycle. Brightly colored. It was the perfect toy for them. The moment I laid eyes on that motorcycle, I knew that I had to buy it for them.

It wasn't expensive—about $1.40 in today's currency. But which child had $1.40 back then? Not I. Nevertheless, I was not about to let the fact that I didn't have money get in the way of my dream. I began to save up. Sometimes the Satmar Rebbetzin would come to visit. When she did, she'd usually slip me a few coins before she left. It took some time and it meant forgoing all candies, but in the end I managed to raise the full amount.

I walked to the toy store on wings of excitement.

The man behind the counter stared at me over his bushy

mustache, probably wondering why no adult had accompanied me into his shop.

"What do you want, little girl?"

Wordlessly I gestured at the row of toy motorcycles parked on the counter, and pointed firmly to the red one. I could already see my brothers zooming it all over their cell, making eager engine sounds and forgetting where they were for a few happy minutes.

He picked up the motorcycle in his work-callused hands and placed it in a little bag. Then he held out his hand, the intent of the international gesture unmistakable. I counted my pennies into it. My next visit to the jail couldn't come fast enough.

"Usher and Chaskel Duvid, do I have a surprise for you!"

They were rather apathetic by then. I held the motorcycle inside my fist, teasing them with the knowledge that I had something fun for them hidden inside my palm.

They woke up as if from a stupor.

"What is it?"

"Show us, show us!" they clamored.

Wordlessly I opened my fist, and watched their eyes light up when they saw the gaily painted plaything. They hadn't had a toy in so long. It was almost as if they'd forgotten what a toy even was.

They didn't know what to say. They were speechless—grateful beyond belief. They stared into my eyes with such thankfulness that I was embarrassed. And then they began to play with the red motorcycle. Usher played. Chaskel Duvid played. Another Polish boy who was in their cell played with them, too.

And from what I understand, even the grown-up Jewish prisoners in the jail took a turn with that motorcycle.

I'd given up all my treats, and more, to buy them that

toy, but it had been worth it. Beyond a doubt, it had been worth it. Just for the look in their eyes.

That's the power of love.

———»•«———

I discovered, later on, that Rav Yoel Teitelbaum—the Satmar Rebbe, a relative of ours and a man beloved by millions around the world—had been the main force behind the efforts to get my brothers released from prison. His sense of urgency had made it imperative. The same urgency that categorized every move he made throughout his long and fruitful life.

And when Usher and Chaskel Duvid were finally redeemed, Rav Yoel adopted them as his own and took them in to live with him.

———»•«———

In early 1944, the Munkatcher Rebbe's dream of escape finally came true when a slim window of opportunity opened up, enabling him to rescue his family from what was to become the blazing inferno of Hungarian Jewry and transport them to Eretz Yisrael by ship.

This was one of the only ships that the British officially allowed into Palestine. The vast majority of the other ships running the British blockade of Palestine approached the shores of Eretz Yisrael stealthily, doing their utmost to evade the British Navy that patrolled the Mediterranean with precision and skill. The British Navy almost always managed to uphold the blockade against these incoming vessels.

Rav Baruch tried his utmost to get me on that boat, but it was not to be. Space was extremely limited and he wasn't even able to get his own sister aboard. As I watched the Rabinovitch family leave Budapest, the sorrow in my heart threatened to engulf me. First, because they were my family now. They had treated me like a daughter, with love, caring, compassion, and open arms. And secondly, because I knew deep inside that they were making the right move, and that everything was going to collapse around us in the very near future.

How did I know this?

Why was I so sure?

Because I'd seen the Germans in action. For several years now, they had been honing their skills at decimating whole Jewish populations.

Hungary was next — and by now the Nazis knew exactly what to do.

CHAPTER THIRTEEN

MEANWHILE, MY SISTER DEVORA HAD ARRIVE-din Budapest and had taken up residence at the home of our Aunt Rivchu, Rav Shloma'le Bobover's sister. Sweet Aunt Rivchu.

The house was a peaceful oasis in the middle of the bustling city. Thick carpeting. Velvet drapery from ceiling to floor. Just sitting there was soothing. The fact that the Munkatcher Rebbe and his entire family had managed to escape meant that I'd been left without a home. Aunt Rivchu welcomed me with open arms.

My sister had been in Czechoslovakia and had managed to reach Hungary without getting caught. That took talent. She was the type of person who knew how to accomplish any task to which she set her mind (something that is still true to this day). But she wasn't satisfied with the fact that we were now in Hungary, far away from the savage butchery that was taking place all over Poland. She trusted no one. And even though Budapest seemed like a safe, pleasant place to remain until the war's end, Devora decided that we had better get ourselves over the border and into Romania.

That was easier said than done.

One didn't attempt to cross borders without knowing the perfect route. That meant using guides. And even with guides leading the escape parties, half the time everyone in the escape party was caught and killed, including the guides. Being a guide was like playing Russian roulette. You never knew when someone would press the trigger, and BOOM!

Our first problem was getting to the guides.

That meant connections. And making those connections were a hit-or-miss proposition. You could be lucky and meet just the right person, who would introduce you to another person with links to the underground, which could set up an escape route for the right price. But you could just as easily meet the wrong person: someone who heard you out, promised you assistance, and then took your money and arranged for the Germans to catch you in the act.

That was why you had to be so careful, every step of the way. Because there were no second chances.

Devora knew all this. Luckily for us, we had a whole team of very smart people to give us advice and guidance, including the Satmar Rebbetzin and the Munkatcher Rebbetzin before she left. We had a network on whom to rely, people capable of finding us a trustworthy guide to smuggle us over the border and into Romania.

The first step in getting to Romania was traveling to a town that was close to the Romanian border. That was why Devora came to the conclusion that it was high time we went to Klausenberg. She wasted no time. Just a few days later we had arrived in Klausenberg, where Devora left me with the guide who was supposed to escort me over the border on the morrow.

Meanwhile, Devora returned to Satmar to bring my brothers to Klausenberg as well. We had lost enough of our family already. My sister would do her impressive best to ensure that the remnants were saved.

———◦◦◦———

Klausenberg was a tiny, picturesque town made up of a few streets and a railroad station. There was mud everywhere. And the cold —! Hungary may not be as bad as other countries in Eastern Europe when it comes to frigid winters, but it's no seaside resort. A bitter cold enveloped the town, like numbing tentacles stretching in every direction, determined to take control.

I shuddered, and not only with the cold. I'd already been smuggled over one border, and the experience had not been a good one. My fear was intense.

Not long before, Klausenberg had been a spiritual fortress, with Chassidim making their way from all across Hungary to the home of the Klausenberger Rebbe for *berachos* and advice. These days, if you didn't absolutely have to travel you stayed where you were. But that didn't mean that people weren't still coming to Klausenberg. They just weren't coming for the same reasons as those who had come previously. Now the town was full of those who were hoping to escape.

The guide was a quiet man. Tall and rugged, he gave off an aura of immense physical strength. The kind of strength it took to soldier people across mountains and rivers while avoiding Nazi patrols eager to send people to their final destination.

I'd seen my fair share of guides by now. None had let me down so far. I was hoping for the best this time, too. A religious Jewish couple were heading to Romania as well. They were going to have to split up because I had come there first and the guide could take only two people at a time.

It's very difficult for me to tell you what happened next.

The husband pulled the guide aside and made him an offer.

"I know the price we agreed on," he told the guide, "but I would like to raise the offer. According to the original agreement, my wife and I were to have been split up, with one of us and the little girl going first. I will pay you double if you take us first and leave her behind."

I can't really fault the guide for accepting the tempting offer. He was risking his life, and probably felt that he deserved every last *pengo*. But once again, a *frum Yid* was trying to take advantage of a young, helpless child who was on her own with no parents to take care of her.

I had grown up seeing the inherent goodness in people: my parents, my grandparents, my cousins and aunts and uncles. Now I was seeing people who came from the same background as I, people who had been religious their entire lives and would have never considered eating *treife*. Yet they didn't hesitate over leaving a child behind, even though she had the first right to leave.

I never forgot the sense of betrayal I felt then. These people were my brothers —

It was a terrible feeling that left a permanent mark.

⸺❖⸺

I was left behind in the guide's house with another couple, the husband's sister and the guide's surly wife. She wasn't very good company, but I had no interest in talking to anyone anyway. All I wanted was to leave this miserable house, with its stench of non-kosher food, and smuggle over the border.

Don't worry, I told myself. *The guide will be back soon, and then it would be your turn.*

I waited all afternoon on pins and needles for news, any news. Night arrived. I cowered in my room, unable to sleep.

My fertile imagination flew every which way, imagining the worst.

Next morning there came a banging on the door. I had experienced enough by then to have developed a sixth sense about things. When I heard those pounding fists, I knew, I just knew, that the worst had happened.

The guide's wife opened the door.

Another man was standing in the doorway. A peasant/guide, just like her husband. He was white as a sheet.

"What's the matter?" she demanded almost belligerently. Apparently, what she had worried about for so long had finally happened.

"He made it across the border all right," the man said. "But he was caught on the way back."

She almost collapsed.

"Is he —?"

The man made a motion with his hand which I interpreted correctly as meaning that the woman's husband was no longer among the living. As soon as he'd relayed the news he was gone, probably afraid to remain there any longer then he had to. The house had become a danger zone, and he wasn't prepared to stay.

I watched my hostess visibly pull herself together. She couldn't afford to fall apart now. There would be time for that later. Right now, she had to get me out of her house.

Within minutes, she'd gotten in touch with members of the Klausenberg Jewish community, who arrived to direct us to a new place of refuge, where we would wait until another guide could be found to do the job.

And so, I lost my opportunity to cross the border to a couple who were willing to pay more and to take what was not rightfully theirs.

We were installed in the home of Klausenberg's *shochet.*

He was a fine Jew, and a prominent member of his community. He was also a man who didn't have a clue about what was about to happen to Hungarian Jewry.

I was at a standstill. I'd been counting on going with my guide into Romania. Now my guide was no more, and I had no idea what to do next. I was very young—still a child. And, for once, this child was feeling completely overwhelmed.

But even if I didn't know where to turn, there were other adults in the *shochet's* house with me who had connections and were prepared to make use of them. They would know what to do. The only option, it seemed, was for them to agree to take me along when they attempted the border crossing.

We sat in the *shochet's* living room, each of us having staked out a spot against a wall or on the couch. A roaring fire lit up the room. Though the blaze warmed us physically, our hearts remained stone-cold because the fear of tomorrow wouldn't leave us. I inched toward the fireplace, desperate for the extra warmth. I had to ask them. I was fearful that they would refuse, but hoping that they would take pity on me.

I was just a little girl.

Surely they could see that?

Were they capable of leaving me behind? I wouldn't have thought so, but after what had occurred the day before I wasn't sure about anything anymore. A portion of my innocent trust in humanity had died the first time I'd overheard that mother in the forest trying to convince the guide to take her and her son first. And now it had happened again, except that this time it was infinitely worse. The Jewish couple had gone. They had made it to the other side. The guide had been killed—and I? I'd been left behind.

It was a freezing night. The wind was moaning outside the house as if mad with worry over what the morning would bring. Nobody felt ready to leave the warmth of the living room and go to bed. Safety was in numbers, and the numbers were in the living room.

I turned to the couple.

"Can I ask you for a favor?"

They knew me. They knew my family, and especially my Zeide, Reb Shaya'le. In normal times, they would have treated me like a princess. But these were not normal times. Now I needed them.

"What do you want, sweetheart?"

"I'm begging you to please take me with you when you leave here. I'm begging you not to leave me behind. Can you promise me that you won't leave me behind? Please?"

"Why are you so worried?"

"Why am I so worried?" I was astonished. "Let me see — Maybe it's because everyone I thought I could rely on has deserted me."

A long look passed between the couple. As they conferred with their eyes, I knew, deep in the pit of my stomach, that that look didn't bode well for me. There have been many times when I've known things even though I didn't want to know them. This was one of those times.

No matter how I tried to believe them when they reassured me that they wouldn't leave me behind, a part of me knew that they were not going to take me with them. They were afraid that I would slow them down.

I sat on that living-room floor the entire night, as eventually everyone in the room fell asleep.

And when I awoke, I saw that my worst dreams had come true. The others weren't there anymore. Somehow they had managed to flee during the night, without waking me.

They were gone. Off to Romania, all three of them—on their way to freedom. While I'd been left behind to survive the war on my own.

Believe me when I say that these were the worst parts of my war.

———•◦•———

The *shochet* was staring at me with an apologetic look on his distinguished face. He'd seen them leave, but what could he do? Wake me up so I could argue with them? They didn't want to take me!

He looked at me, kindness and bewilderment mingling, as if he was trying to figure out what was going on in this crazy world we now inhabited.

"You can stay with us for as long as you want. Whatever happens to us will happen to you."

I hated the sound of those words. They were so defeatist. As if he had already accepted that the Nazis were going to kill them all. I, however, was not ready to roll over and play dead.

I shook my head at him. "No."

"No?"

"No. I refuse to wait for the Germans to arrive. I know that my sister was planning on coming back soon with my younger brothers, but I'm not staying here. It seems that everyone knows it's only a matter of time before the Germans come. I must be gone before that happens!" I bit my lip. "The only thing that bothers me is the fact that my sister will be returning from Satmar straight into the trap, because it sounds like the Germans will be here momentarily — Still, I cannot remain!"

It was morning. Time to leave. I had one priority: getting away from Klausenberg alive. I removed any identifying marks that showed I was Jewish. I was leaving with no yellow star. No anything. The gentiles would have to work at catching me.

"Can I please have some money so I can purchase a ticket to Budapest?"

The *shochet* gave me as much as he could spare. I will never forget him. He owed me nothing, yet he did what he could.

"Where are you running to?"

"I will try to get across the border to Romania."

He was impressed by my courage.

Suddenly, his little daughter spoke up. "I want to escape with her!"

The *shochet* shook his head. "My darling daughter," he said, "whatever happens to us will happen to you. You are staying with your family."

She did not make it through the war. In the end, only the *shochet* survived.

———✦———

The *shochet* lived in a private home a few houses away from the corner. There was a long patch of garden between the front door and the street. I flung open the door, determined to put some distance between myself and the house. As I walked through the garden, my fingers worked to blend in the spot on my coat that had been hidden beneath my star. I didn't want it to be immediately obvious that a star had been there until about five minutes ago.

I was scraping at the spot with my nails when I heard a horse and wagon approaching up the street.

I didn't stop to think. I didn't wonder who the driver was, or whether he might give me up to the Germans. The time for reflection was over. Now it was time to operate on instinct and *siyata d'Shmaya*.

I raced through the garden, my hair whipping in the early morning wind and my mind filled with images of a peasant driving a buggy. And that was exactly what I saw. A burly peasant sat on a high seat, driving his cart down the street. I knew that I had to get on that wagon. He was a man of young middle age, clean shaven, with no expression on his face to mar the blandness.

I ran to the wagon, motioning for him to stop. There was desperation in my eyes. He looked down, and he knew that I would have money to give him.

He pulled to a stop, so suddenly that the sparks flew out from beneath the horses' hooves. The power of money —

It was then that I heard it.

A chilling sound.

I felt goose bumps run over my entire body, as raw fear left a metallic taste in my mouth.

It was the sound of the march. The goose-stepping march that the Nazis loved so much. The march that made them so proud, and us so terrified. It was a sound calculated to inspire fear. A sound that, once heard, could never be forgotten.

I didn't know how far away they were, but that didn't matter: they were close enough. Close enough to make me lose everything.

Now I *knew* that I had to board that wagon.

The driver was moving toward me in front of the house.

The Germans were approaching from the back of the house, almost at the corner where *we would meet* if I didn't get away from this spot at once! Clearly, that peasant had seen the soldiers coming; he'd probably passed them on his way over to the *shochet's* house. And he knew who I was, a Jewish girl coming out of that house — but he stopped anyway. Was it was the lure of the money? Or maybe he was Eliyahu Hanavi? Who knows —

I jumped onto that wagon as if the demons of the netherworld were in furious pursuit, and took a seat in the back, under the hood, trying to pretend that everything was just fine, that I wasn't in the greatest hurry of my life, that my heart wasn't pounding as if it was about to jump clear out of my chest. This was no time to fall apart. I needed to be in complete control of myself.

The driver took off down the street, the horses' hooves thudding with numbing regularity. As we moved past the corner, I looked back and saw a German Wehrmacht patrol turning into the very garden that I had just left mere seconds before!

They had not been far away. They hadn't even been a block away. They had been just around the corner, and moving inexorably toward me. Do you have any idea what that felt like?

It felt like the *Yad Hashem* patting my cheek. I had left mere seconds before the Nazis arrived. A few more seconds in the house, in the doorway, or on the street, and that would have been the end of everything.

The wagon drove off, taking me away from the German patrol that was placing the *shochet* and his family under arrest in those same moments. Klausenberg was such a tiny town that it wasn't long before we were approaching the train station. Then I spotted two people I knew. Both were dressed like gentiles. One was a relative of mine. The other was Rabbi Shapiro, the Belzer Rebbe's *gabbai* in Bochnia. I recognized both of them instantly.

I climbed down from the wagon.

I paid the driver, and stood watching for a second as he slipped the cash into his pocket, then whipped the horses with a gentle flick and was off.

I stood outside the station. My first and most urgent need was more money. The *shochet* had given me what he was able to spare, but I urgently needed more. That was why I decided to approach that pair of Jews. They were pretending to be Christians, so I spoke to them in Polish. I told them two things.

First, that I needed money desperately!

And, second: if they happened to run into my sister Devora, they should tell her that the gentile guide had taken someone else ahead of me and gotten himself killed in the process, so I'd been forced to flee Klausenberg for the big city.

My destination was the Roth family, in Budapest.

The Roths were extremely close to the Satmar Rebbe, but like many Chassidim who were either Satmar or Belz, they considered themselves to be Sanzer Chassidim as well. That made them my Zeide's Chassidim. I knew that they would treat me like a daughter.

The two men gave me money.

Once again, I had met precisely whom I needed to meet so I could receive the assistance that was vital for a successful escape.

So I was escaping from Klausenberg to Budapest, while my sister was returning to Klausenberg from Budapest at the exact same time. The irony was not lost on me.

With the money clenched tightly in my fist, I bade the two men farewell and headed into the station to purchase a ticket for the next available train. The ticket seller looked out from his barred enclosure with the suspiciousness so characteristic of Europeans of a certain age. His bushy eyebrows and thick mustache glared at me in silent accusation as he told me the price in a grudging voice.

I handed over the money.

He pushed the ticket through the grate and pocketed the cash.

Holding my ticket gratefully, I walked down the platform trying to decide where to sit for a journey that would take the entire night and half the following day. Choosing the perfect carriage was crucial to making it through this ordeal alive. The wrong carriage meant being surrounded by hostile Hungarians who desired nothing more than to hand people like me over to their Nazi masters on a silver platter.

When I tell you that *Hashem* was guiding me every step of the way, I am in no way exaggerating. I felt His presence beside me. I knew He was there! The next move I made was not something I could attribute to any exceptional clarity or clairvoyance on my part. It came about solely by virtue of my putting my complete trust in *Hashem*, taking the backseat and allowing Him to guide me. I just went where He told me to go.

I walked the length of the platform, passing carriage after carriage, each one filled with gentiles ready and waiting to hand me over to the Germans. Which carriage should I enter? What should I do?

The next move I made was completely unexpected—even by me. Someone else had taken over and was instructing me, step by step.

Go into the first carriage, the voice told me.

I took a good look inside the first carriage. There were two blond German soldiers sitting near the front of the car. I do not know what possessed me to board the very carriage where my mortal enemies sat comfortably with each other, sharing a joke with the ease of victors. My brain screamed at me to run the other way, to board the last carriage, but my heart told me to do exactly the opposite of what reason demanded.

I boarded the carriage that held the enemy.

Not only did I board the carriage with the German soldiers, but I made my way down the aisle, past the people sitting on either side of that train compartment, until I reached the front where the Nazi soldiers sat, directly across from each other on opposite sides of the aisle. I slipped unceremoniously into a seat right beside one of them, as if this was the most natural choice of seating arrangement in the world. Right beside those nice, young, blond boys, those perfect Aryan specimens.

They were very young soldiers. Hungary was probably their first posting. Lucky for them. Otherwise, they would almost certainly have been dead by now, killed by a Russian bullet or an American shell. I assumed they were homesick, missing their mothers and their little sisters, because they gave me big smiles and welcomed me to their section of the train. I accepted their kindness enthusiastically and proceeded to charm them with the very few German words at my disposal.

Don't waste time on words! my inner voice urged.

Why? I wondered. *What should I do instead?*

Suddenly, I knew.

I should sing.

It so happened that my mother had enjoyed singing to me in German when I was very little. She came from a city that had belonged to the Germans at one time, so she knew the language and, more importantly, had taught me how to sing in it. In fact, I knew some lullabies that were guaranteed to find their way right into the heart of any true German.

I opened my mouth and began to sing.

I sang a song about a bird that came to me with a note in its beak, bringing regards from my mother.

"I can't stay here, I must fly back to your mother — Little bird, fly back to my mother/I'm so sorry, but I must remain here —" (As very roughly translated from the German.)

The young soldiers joined in at the refrain. I sang the lyrics and they'd swoop in for the chorus, singing loudly and enthusiastically.

"Little bird, fly back to my mother/I'm so sorry, but I must remain here —"

Were those tears in their eyes when they sang about having to remain where they were? Did they miss their homes that much? Or were they just afraid of the battles that lay ahead?

The smiles that came to those boyish faces when I started to sing cannot be described. They just lit up. Those soldiers were transformed. I could see their faces glowing with memories of home and a tender mother's love.

They asked me questions, and I did my best to understand them and respond in sign language. Then, as the train picked up speed and began racing down the tracks, I spied some animals grazing in the distance and began copying the sounds they made. Our corner of the carriage was suddenly filled with a variety of animal sounds. I bellowed out a wide assortment of *moos*, followed by *baas* and *maas* when we saw some sheep and goats a little later on. Those soldiers found me absolutely hilarious. Soon we were seeing who could *moo* better, and the sounds of our mirth and merriment filled the train. I was happy, even though I felt so scared and sad at the same time.

I had become an actress. It was as simple as that. I was playing a part.

A part that, quite simply, saved my life.

I wasn't the only one who ran away from Klausenberg on that fateful morning. Far from it. Everyone was try to escape Klausenberg that morning, because the Nazis had just arrived—and if the Nazis were in Klausenberg, then Klausenberg was no longer a safe place for Jews. So the trains were packed with people either pretending to be gentiles, or Jews who didn't even pretend but were trying to run away as well. Needless to say, it was not a good day for any Jew attempting to slip away without arousing suspicion.

And here I was, attempting to do exactly that.

Looking back, I have no idea how I managed to get past all the security. It was intense. It wasn't even that there were so many German soldiers; Hitler's Army, busy fighting on two fronts, was spread a little thin. But the Hungarians more than made up for the Nazis' sparse presence. The Hungarian Arrow Cross were a group of fanatical anti-Semites who ably assisted the Nazis in all their vicious plans, and they were overjoyed at the opportunity for mass murder that had finally come their way long after the rest of Europe had had their chance at killing Jews. At last it was their turn, and they went at it with a single-mindedness that told of long-stifled desires finally unleashed.

It was those beasts, even more than the Germans, who were waiting by the train station and all around the town, intent on catching any Jew attempting to escape. And I had managed to evade a Nazi patrol by seconds, had made it onto the train undetected, and was sitting in the company of a couple of Nazi soldiers, making animal sounds for their amusement and singing them lullabies.

The Germans were at a slight disadvantage when it came to the Hungarian Jewish public, since they didn't speak the language and the Jews were able to act as if they didn't understand them. Enter the Arrow Cross, who knew exactly what to say to determine whether someone was Jewish or not. All they needed to do was ask every Jew they met to recite some of the Catholic catechism in Latin. Because, needless to say, we did not know their religious prayers. We had never learned what every good Hungarian child had memorized at an early age. This was an almost foolproof way of tracking down Jews. And that's why a day that had begun extremely badly was continuing to grow even worse.

My danger was acute. I knew none of the gentiles' prayers. Not in Hungarian, not in Latin, not in Finnish. I was the great-granddaughter of the Divrei Chaim. I knew *Modeh Ani*, not Christian liturgy. Not only was I unfamiliar with their prayers, I didn't even speak Hungarian. If an officer of the Arrow Cross chose to interrogate me, he would know instantly what I was. There would be no question in his mind.

It was the ultimate recipe for disaster.

I was riding a train filled with fleeing Jews and Arrow Cross men poised to interrogate anyone who appeared at all suspicious, and I knew virtually no Hungarian and even less Latin. Already I could see Arrow Cross officers going from carriage to carriage. Soon they would reach me!

Suddenly, I started up and stared. What were they doing?

I watched in horror as they selected a victim.

"Stand up."

(It was so hard to concentrate on my singing for the soldiers when a fellow Jew was being interrogated at the other end of the carriage.)

It was a young Jew. I couldn't get a clear picture of exactly how old he was, but judging by the sound of his voice he couldn't have been more than fifteen or sixteen.

"Recite for us in Latin."

The boy never had a chance. Of course he couldn't do that.

The Hungarians stopped the train, as if they'd discovered a terrible criminal who needed to be transferred to jail as soon as humanly possible. And then they began to beat him, right there in the middle of the train. All around, the other passengers watched impassively.

"Jew, you're trying to escape! As if we would let you get away!

"Go on—say your prayers in Latin —"

They hurt him badly, but I couldn't even cry out in

sympathy. And then they threw him off the train and followed him down, and there began the beating of a lifetime. As long as I live, I will never forget that boy's screams. And I couldn't even look out the window, because that would have given me away.

The train waited —

Eventually, the crying stopped.

The Hungarians re-boarded — without the boy. He was dead. They had killed him and left his body alongside the train tracks, in the middle of nowhere.

And now they were on the lookout for more Jews to terrorize. I almost stopped breathing. Would it be my turn next?

———✦———

They were in my carriage now, headed my way. I didn't know what to do. What would *you* have done? All they needed to do was ask me a question, and they'd immediately know who I was.

They had almost reached my seat. My mouth was completely dry and my heart hammered loudly in my chest. A raging headache pounded at my brain, making it impossible to think. This was it. In just a second or two, they would find me out.

My next move came directly from *Hashem*. There is no other way to look at it.

I am a granddaughter of Reb Shaya'le, youngest son of the Divrei Chaim of Sanz. In the past, growing up, I would have never dreamed of putting my hand on any of my boy cousins, even when we were playing together as eight-year-olds. But now I did something that went against every fiber of my being.

Somehow, I knew that this was what I was supposed to do at that moment. The young Nazi soldier was sitting beside me on the hard train seat. His companion was seated on the bench opposite us. As the officers of the Arrow Cross came too close for comfort, looking my way as if determined to question me, I laid down on the bench and put my head on the soldier's knees the way a younger sister might do. The soldier did not protest. Rather, he began talking to me much as he probably talked to his younger sister back home in Stuttgart, or Munich, or wherever he was from.

I was able to peek out from under his arm and see the entire compartment.

The men from the Arrow Cross were almost upon us now, and one of them opened his mouth, probably to order me to sit up and take the Latin test. Then the soldier from across the aisle picked up his hand (I watched him do this from under the shelter of the first soldier's arm) and motioned angrily for them to go away and not bother us.

The Arrow Cross officer had his orders and was anxious to carry them out, but he knew as well as everyone else that it was not worth his while to start up with the Nazis. If one of them was telling him to get away from this little girl, then that was exactly what he would do. He nodded stiffly, and moved away.

The fact that I'd instinctively acted as I had is something that astounds me to this day. It went against everything in my nature, everything in my upbringing. But this was the move that *Hashem* put in my mind to save my life. And it worked.

A few more minutes passed, and then I bounded up off my neighbor's knees like a typical child. The soldiers smiled and laughed because I was so cute. And once again we were singing songs, making animal noises, and doing all the things they found so amusing. This was my ticket out of Klausenberg.

This was the hand of G-d, from start to finish.

From the start of this incredible journey, I'd acted against all reason, and against my own nature. It was completely out of character for me to contemplate joining a pair of German soldiers in their carriage.

Astounding for me to make friends with my greatest enemies.

Most amazing of all was the fact that that German soldier had responded by treating me like his sister!

There was only one way to look at all of this. *Hashem* had taken me by the hand, so to speak, and had drawn me after Him. He'd issued clear instructions: *Do this; now do that.*

And I did them, and I was saved. Because that was what *Hashem* wanted to happen.

Sometimes I wonder —

Could those two soldiers really have been Jewish boys, dressed up in German uniforms and pretending to be Nazis? I imagine myself tracking them down through the endless war archives. I imagine asking them why they acted as they did.

We are always in *Hashem's* hands—but on that particular train ride it was astonishingly clear that I was being guided, every step of the way.

I will never know who those soldiers really were. Just another one of the mysteries of the world that will never be solved.

<hr />

The train chugged along, rapidly making its way down the track through hill and dale, past fields full of flowers in every color of the rainbow, the occasional vineyard and pastures dotted with grazing cows and running dogs. The sun had woken up and the whole world shone.

Hungary is a breathtaking country, I thought to myself. *If only it were a little bit more beautiful in the way it treats its Jewish citizens —*

As day gave way to evening, our conversation came to a stop as we drifted off into dreamland. The light outside the window faded, and soon enough all was dark outside and I could see nothing. My stomach rumbled with hunger, but I made no sign that I was uncomfortable. It didn't matter in the slightest. Hunger meant nothing to me in those days. My life was on the line.

And then my chin descended gently onto my chest, and I slept.

I dreamed the hours away in the carriage, where the wary silence was punctuated by the occasional snore from a fellow passenger.

From time to time I woke up, my eyes accustomed to the gloom of the dimly lit carriage. The night seemed endless. But it finally passed, as night always does. Soon enough, the sky outside the window was turning a rosy shade of pink and orange. And then, at long last, we arrived at the Budapest station.

My soldier companions grabbed their bags, and I gave them a wave and a mischievous grin as we exchanged good-byes. I knew that they had enjoyed their time with me more than almost anything they'd experienced in the last few months. I had given them a taste of home, and they were properly appreciative.

I felt the same way toward them. After all, they had saved my life.

———◦———

The Budapest train station was, as always, a cosmopolitan wonderland. People streamed by in every direction. All sorts of people: big and little, fat and skinny, military and civilian, loud and silent, happy and morose, drunk and sober. I waited until the Germans had moved away and out of my life, and then walked through the station trying to decide on my next move. It would have to be a good one.

My nerves were stretched taut, and I was exhausted. It had been a long day.

I'd left Klausenberg and embarked on a hair-raising journey—barely evading the Nazi patrol at the *shochet's* front door, hitching a ride to the station, taking a seat right beside two German soldiers, and miraculously being left alone by the Arrow Cross. At long last, I'd reached my destination.

Now I was faced with another problem.

To get out of the station at Budapest, you had to show your ticket to a policeman stationed at the great front doors. I had a ticket; the problem was getting past the German military cop and the Hungarian officers beside him, without having them pull me over and throw me in jail.

What to do? Had I come this far, only to get caught in the final lap of the race?

I looked around desperately, trying to decide what to do. From whence would my salvation come? From the corner of my eye I could see the officers at the giant doors, checking every person who passed and making sure they could legitimately be allowed through to join the unsuspecting public. I could hear a polite voice over the loudspeaker, announcing departures and arrivals, as I wondered, *What to do? What to do?* Was it all going to end here?

No. A second later, I knew just what to do.

There was a businessman walking across the concourse. He was in a hurry, not pausing to look in any direction. He was focused on reaching the doorway and the street. Probably he had some meeting to attend in the city. He wore a trench coat with an unfastened belt hanging down carelessly close to the floor. He was too busy to even notice, which worked perfectly for my purposes.

I stepped smartly up behind him and picked up the dangling end of that unfastened belt. If you didn't know better, you could be forgiven for imagining that it was my father's belt I was holding. And I cradled it so gently in my hands that the man didn't even realize I was there.

The military cop thought exactly what I'd hoped he would. The man passed him his ticket and the cop waved him through without a word. And I walked through as well—right behind him. I handed one of the officers my ticket as I went past. He accepted it, no questions asked.

Nobody challenged me. They just assumed I was with my father. (I had so many "fathers" in those years.) And that's how I managed to leave the Budapest train station intact.

I stepped outside to face the uncertain future.

CHAPTER FOURTEEN

I DON'T REALLY KNOW HOW I REACHED THE ROTH home. It all seemed like a dream as I walked the streets of Budapest, miraculously still free after a day and a night that, by rights, should have had me on a train to the Polish killing grounds by now.

I made my careful way through the center of the city, toward Pest and the apartment where I hoped to stay. It was a distinguished-looking building with a brick facade. There was a doorman. Flowers had been planted around the perimeter of the building. Fashionable women walked dogs in well-bred silence, noses in the air, ignoring anyone not from their social class. The lobby was elegant—a far cry from Klausenberg, and certainly from the Sucha of my youth.

My youth? By this time, although I may still have been technically young in years, I was feeling far from youthful. I was an old person hiding in a child's body. I had seen too much, been shot at and threatened too many times. Been abandoned by those I trusted and those I hadn't trusted.

I climbed the stairs, my feet sinking into the carpet. The lighting was muted, the sounds of people going about their everyday business unmistakable and comforting. The door to the apartment was constructed of thick wood and looked as if it could keep the world out. But I knew better. I knew it wouldn't be able to keep out anything.

The apartment was very nice. Apparently, the Roths were well to do. I was warmly welcomed, served a filling meal, and in short order found myself sitting with my host. I told Mr. Roth my entire story, from beginning to end. How I'd just managed to escape by the skin of my teeth. How I didn't know what my sister was doing now, or even where she was. How she had been planning to return to Klausenberg, not knowing that the town was now under Nazi control.

He listened to me, but could offer no immediate solutions. We sat there together, feeling helpless.

———⟫•⟪———

A few days passed. Mrs. Roth walked around the apartment with a stricken look on her face. The stress was terrible. Would the dreaded knock arrive today? Would this be their last day in Budapest?

We were sitting in the living room when it came. At the banging on the door, my hostess's face turned white. Her hands were shaking. I could see how fearful she was. Had the moment arrived at last? Had the Nazis come for us all?

There was no point in prolonging the inevitable. I went to see who it was. As I approached the door, I suddenly felt a strange, hopeful feeling that heralded happiness. Something whispered to me that my family stood behind that front door. And, in fact, when I peered through the peephole, I could discern my sister Devora and my two brothers standing in the hall!

I cannot describe my feelings at that moment. I had almost given up hope of ever seeing my family again. What were the chances? They were traveling around Europe on Nazi-infested trains, trying to escape with false documents or none at all. I hadn't been able to fall asleep at night from the fear that I was the sole survivor of my entire family—and now, here they stood. The joy was overwhelming. It was intoxicating!

I had told myself that if my sister and the boys don't make it, I was finished running as well. I had come to the end of my rope. I refused to run anymore.

But here they were. I suddenly felt as if I could run again. I could run to the ends of the earth if need be. It was a liberating feeling. It was a new lease on life.

———◦◦◦———

Now that my sister had stepped back into my life, I gratefully reverted to my role of little sister. I knew that Devora was incredibly talented at making connections with people who were able to get things done. I could finally step out of the picture and stop making decisions. And Devora didn't let me down. Soon enough, she met someone who promised to be of service to us.

I will never know his name.

To me, he will always be the tall man with the broad shoulders from Sucha who knew about Rudolf Kastner and the special train he was organizing: a train that would transport hundreds of Jews out of Budapest.

Kastner had made a deal with the Nazis, who apparently respected him a great deal and were prepared to honor any agreements made with the Zionist government's man in Budapest. The train, which was to be filled with the rich and famous of Hungary, would supposedly be traveling to Switzerland. Everyone wanted to be on that train. Everyone.

Much has been written about Rudolf Kastner. He would go on to survive the war, move to Israel, and become one of the movers and shakers in the earliest government of Ben-Gurion. He was a multitalented linguist, an affable personality blessed with fascinating oratory abilities and excellent diplomatic skills. He received a very respectable job working for the State of Israel after the war. He was on his way up—on personal terms with all the top men in the Israeli government. He could see the foreign office from his window.

Until, that is, one Malkiel Gruenwald made his lonely voice heard.

Malkiel Gruenwald owned a small hotel on Jerusalem's Jaffa Road, right across the street from Ben Yehuda Street. He was nobody rich, nobody famous—really, nobody at all. And then, one day, Gruenwald, who fancied himself an amateur journalist, printed an article that accused Rudolf Kastner of collaborating with the Nazis.

Nothing would have come of his accusations, were it not for the fact that the State of Israel sued Gruenwald for defamation of character—a trial that would go on to destroy Kastner for all time, as the people of Israel learned things about their leaders and their government that they would much rather have never known. Gruenwald was represented by Shmuel Tamir, former head of the Irgun in Jerusalem and fierce critic of Ben-Gurion and his cronies in the Mapai party. The trial was covered by the world media. One reporter for the New York Times, a man by the name of Ben Hecht, even wrote a book about it.

He called it *Perfidy*.

The book was banned in Israel for many years. The Israeli government even wrote a critique on the book, which was sold along with the actual manuscript.

What was the end of Kastner, that heroic rescuer of so

few of Hungary's Jews? He was shot by an unknown assailant on a motorcycle as he was exiting his home one morning.

Was he an evil man? Was he a good man? I don't know. There seems to be a disagreement among the historians on that point. But we were not looking at Kastner from the vantage point of history. Our lives were on the line. Should I feel bad that we desperately wanted to board a train that had room for mere hundreds, when thousands would be left behind?

I was only a child. I don't have the answers to all these weighty questions. All I knew at the time was that there was a train being organized and that maybe, just maybe, we would be able to acquire tickets, although that would mean using all our connections. But weren't connections meant for exactly this type of situation?

"Who will be able to get on this train?" Devora asked the big man from Sucha. "It sounds as if it's only meant for rich and influential individuals."

"That's true. But your family is related to everyone. All the key people. All the big rebbes. I have no doubt that I can manage to secure tickets for your family."

He introduced her to some of the people on the Kastner committee. It wasn't an easy process, and truthfully this is a part of my story about which I don't have complete clarity, simply because I had stepped out of the decision-making process and reverted to the role of docile little sister. In the end, however, Devora managed to get hold of tickets for the four of us on that train.

Me? I didn't believe that train would ever be allowed to reach Switzerland. That would mean, first, that the Germans were telling the truth about something (almost an impossibility for them) and second, that they would be allowing

Jews to live (again, something that went against a very deep part of their psyche and philosophy). But everyone else seemed to trust them. I had finally been reunited with my family, and if this was what they wanted to do, then I was going to do it alongside them.

And if we were to perish, it would be in the company of some of the richest, most influential, most prominent and upstanding members of our nation.

I could think of worse ways to go.

———⇒◦⇐———

My sister and I were issued tickets for the train in the names of two girls who for some unknown reason had not arrived. Everything was truly a matter of *mazal* and *hashgachah* back then. Those girls had managed to secure reservations, yet they didn't arrive to claim them.

They could have been saved, if only they'd boarded that train. That's all it would have taken.

But we were the ones meant to board that day.

Devora and I traveled under the name Rosenkrantz, and the boys went under Halberstam.

And that's how we journeyed to Bergen-Belsen.

Everyone knew that the Kastner train was going to the Bergen-Belsen concentration camp. The novelty was that people actually believed the Germans when they promised that it would continue on to Switzerland from there. But desperate people are willing to believe anything. To believe is to hope, and without hope what does anyone have?

Personally, I never believed them. How could I believe the animals who had put me through such *Gehinnom* for the past few years?

They'd shot at me as if I was a rabbit.

They'd locked me up in prisons.

Tried to corner me in Klausenberg.

Caused my sister to starve to death.

Killed my parents and Zeide Shaya'le.

I had been forced to endure gnawing hunger in the forests and mountains for days on end because of them.

There was no way that I could ever trust the Nazis about anything. Ever.

But it didn't matter, because I was past all that. Nothing really mattered to me anymore.

The Kastner train departed Budapest for points unknown with four Halberstams on board. Four children.

Ki avi v'imi azavani, v'Hashem ya'asfeni — for my father and mother have abandoned me, but *Hashem* will gather me in — He will stand by me, supporting me —

Now what? I couldn't summon up the interest to really care. The train began picking up speed, taking us past the beautiful and artistically designed homes of Hungary's capital, past the pedestrians with their well-dressed children and nannies, past the stores still selling luxury items.

Now we were out of the city. There were no more houses. We were crossing bridges over deep gorges and lakes, where men in straw hats fished with their feet dangling over the sides of their boats, their lines trailing lazily in the water. We swept in and out of villages, the main streets flying by like speeding bullets.

I gazed out at the villages we passed, and wondered: Were there Jews hiding in those villages, dreading the Nazi noose that was slowly tightening around their necks?

Hours passed. It was a long way to Germany. I felt as if everything was coming full circle. Mother had grown up singing German children's songs, and now here we were, coming back to the place where it had all begun so long before.

Were we going there to live or to die?

Suddenly the train's wheels began slowing. They gradually ground to a halt.

I broke out in sweat. Why were we stopping? It was the middle of nowhere. Far off in the extreme distance I could see a village—a mere speck on the horizon. Otherwise, the area was completely deserted. The track had been built in the middle of a field. Wildflowers grew here in abundance. Sunflowers raised their pretty, smiling faces to the sky. Lighthearted birds chirped in the trees.

There was nothing here, and yet we were stopping. My heart told me that they were planning to kill us right here! Why should they transport us all the way to Germany if they could get rid of us here and now, in the middle of an empty field?

The wheels ceased their clanking. The train stopped.

"Devora," I whispered. "I have a bad feeling about this."

"Shhh," she replied.

I shrugged. It didn't matter anyway. If they didn't kill us here, they would kill us somewhere else. What difference did it make if someone was killed in Bochnia, Klausenberg, or near some train tracks in the middle of a Hungarian field? No difference at all.

Now the German soldiers were walking alongside the carriages, rifles at the ready. They opened up the siding in the carriages and ordered everyone down and into the fields. Nobody resisted. I didn't even consider disobeying their orders. What could possibly be gained by that?

Strangely, this place didn't look like a killing ground. It was too peaceful. Too beautiful. It didn't make sense. Why transport us all the way here, when they could have shot us on the banks of the Danube, as they had so many thousands of others?

"*Raus, Juden, raus!*" the Germans shouted their orders,

pointing at us and motioning for us to move on toward the center of the field.

It didn't matter that this train contained the wealthiest, most influential families of Budapest. To the Germans, Jews were Jews and should not expect to be treated differently just because they had more money than their brothers. A lesson for life.

All of us went. Rebbes who had commanded flocks of Chassidim numbering in the thousands prior to the war, men who had run international companies with branches around the globe, financiers and diplomats, rabbinical leaders and politicians. All of us together, with those Germans treating us all the same. Wearily we trudged toward the center of the field, where we were finally allowed to stop. We were ordered to lie down and take it easy.

To my shock, it didn't appear that the Germans were planning on killing us today. Maybe tomorrow—but not today. For now, they wanted us to rest and relax. Our death sentence had been temporarily commuted.

———

We rested in that field for a few hours and were then ordered back onto the train, with no explanation as to why we'd been ordered off it in the first place. Ten minutes later the engine was started again. The wheels began to move and soon enough we were back on track: destination, Germany. Bergen-Belsen.

But before we could slide into the tracks at that infamous concentration camp, we had a stop to make. We were going to Munich.

Everyone knows about Munich. If Austria spawned a monster named Hitler, Munich is the place where his infamous career truly began.

This was the city where a crazed Adolf Hitler, commanding a band of power-hungry Nazis, attempted a putsch in 1923. This was the true cradle of Nazism, the birthplace of the dream and the last place a Jew could ever feel comfortable. The train stopped outside the city. Almost as if the Germans had mixed feelings about bringing us into their clean train station. Once again we disembarked, and were marched from the outskirts of the city to our barracks.

It wasn't long before we arrived at a crosswalk that was intersected by trolley tracks. Our masters ordered us to stop. A trolley was coming. We could hear it screech as it moved along. We waited, five abreast in every line, docilely obeying the officers. But I didn't want to obey. I wanted to show the German populace on that trolley just how low they had descended. I wanted to cry out and tell them exactly what I thought of them.

Then we were moving again. Curious Germans watched us walk by.

I was suddenly fired up with a desire to create a scene. To shove their sordid behavior right into the German people's faces. If I stopped walking when ordered to move, the officers would shoot me right in the middle of that Munich street. And then the Germans would see what they had become. How low they had sunk.

"I'm going to stop walking," I whispered to my sister, who was standing in the next row.

The Satmar Rebbetzin noticed what I was doing. She understood that I was in the grip of a spate of temporary insanity. She gave me a hard shove.

"What do you think you're doing?" she hissed through clenched teeth. "Do you really think the Germans are going to be content with shooting just you? They'll shoot us all!"

That was all I needed to hear. I immediately realized that

the Rebbetzin was right. The shove she gave me had been strong enough to pull me back from the brink of disaster.

<hr />

We continued walking through the streets of a city strewn with hate. The people saw us. We were passing right in front of them. There was no way anyone could protest that they didn't know. It's amazing how the populace of Europe tried to claim ignorance of all the travesties that occurred right under their noses, even as they watched innocent prisoners being paraded through the streets of their cities. Watched with hooded eyes and guilty souls.

It wasn't long before we were being led into a complex, where we were ordered to wash ourselves. The Germans claimed that we needed to do this because, if we wanted to be around them, we were going to have to maintain a higher level of hygiene. Of course, they separated the men from the women. It was at that point that I broke down.

Because I knew, I just knew, that this was the last time I was going to see my two brothers.

"Don't you see?" I cried to Devora. "They're taking them away and we'll never see them again! They are taking us to be gassed. It won't be a shower! It will be a gas chamber! "

"It's just a shower." Devora spoke in the calm voice of reason. But I refused to believe her. I knew the Nazis all too well by now.

I was utterly hysterical. My sister knew that this was neither the time nor the place to fall apart. But I was beyond reason. It was as if all the logical thought I'd been capable of until that moment had suddenly dissipated in a cloud of smoke. Finally, my sister approached Reb Yosef Ashkenazy, the Satmar Rebbe's *gabbai*, and asked him to please keep an eye on the boys. And, of course, he agreed.

I calmed down just a little bit.

The next thing I knew, we were being escorted into showers. I looked around that sterile room and knew that everything was about to come to an end, then and there. I waited for the gas to come flowing into the room, where it would cut off my circulation and kill me.

But it didn't come. Instead, to my complete shock and surprise, a wonderful stream of water came surging from the showerheads. We washed in the time allotted us, and then dried off, put back on the same clothes we had arrived in, and once again were on our way back to the train and the continuation of our journey.

Not long after that, we finally arrived at the gates of one of the most infamous of all the Nazi concentration camps: Bergen-Belsen.

———❖———

Bergen-Belsen was our new home. We were quartered in Barracks 10 and half of 11. The other half of Barracks 11 housed Polish prisoners. Here, as well, there were showers nearby which we were ordered to use on a regular basis. This frightened me enormously, because I was never sure when the day would come when the Germans would decide that, instead of water, it was time for the gas.

I was happy that we couldn't run anymore. I was resigned to my fate. We might have been on our way to Switzerland, but we were still surrounded by barbed-wire fences and watch towers, and there were still armed guards with vicious dogs everywhere we looked.

And of course there was still the terrible building with the smoking chimney that sent our brothers and sisters up to heaven every day. It was only natural that I imagined my time would be coming soon as well.

———❖———

There was an older woman with us who had been a teacher back in Poland. She decided that since we had such a vast quantity of free time on our hands, we might as well devote some of it toward structured learning. She began teaching us the letters of the alphabet, math and science, and within a short time we had mastered quite a lot of material. Learning was certainly better than being idle and wasting our time. Even though we had no educational materials, we made the best of the situation.

Years later, I asked her why she did it.

"Nobody cared about anything during the war years, but all you wanted to do was to teach us," I said. "Why?"

"Because then you weren't focusing on your terrible situation," she replied. "You were doing, accomplishing, learning. Above all, you were imagining a future where you might need to use this information—and that was the most important thing of all."

We might have been part of a separate group that was cut off from the main Bergen-Belsen camp, but we still knew the big rule: the Germans had no use for sick people. Going to the infirmary was almost like signing your own death warrant. So we never went. There were times when we were sick and wanted nothing more than to go to a place where we might obtain medicine, but we knew that in a Nazi world, a place for sick people was nothing more than a glorified entryway to the gas chamber.

But then my tooth began acting up. If, at first I was merely uncomfortable, before I knew it terrible pains were shooting all through my head. The tooth was infected. Incredible pain. Swelling. There was a Yugoslavian dentist living in our barrack. He examined the tooth and informed me, in grave tones, that if I did not have it seen to immediately, I was going to die from the infection. It was that simple.

Having no choice in the matter, I informed the officers

in charge of our section of the camp that I needed to see a dentist as soon as possible. And I was in good company. Reb Yosef Ashkenazy, the Satmar *gabbai*, was also suffering terribly from a tooth infection and had decided to submit himself, against his better judgment, to be "healed" by the German dentists of Bergen-Belsen.

So we went.

It was an unforgettable experience—though not in a good way.

Young, ostensibly professional dentists in white lab coats were there to treat us. There were chairs to lean back in, a sink to spit into. It could have been a manageable ordeal. But the dentists were as amateur as was possible to be, and they hadn't a clue how to perform an operation. In the process of cleaning out the pus, they broke my tooth into seven parts! I screamed louder than I've ever screamed before or after. The pain was simply unbearable.

Forget about painkillers. There was nothing like that. Nothing to ease the pain. Those dentists went in with their shovels and dug at my tooth until it cracked, and then they went ahead and cleaned out the infection, never mind the fact that the nerves were exposed and the pain intolerable. I could hear Reb Yosef moaning in agony close by and knew that I was not alone, but that didn't make me feel any better. I felt as if the pain was going to rip me in two.

When we finally finished the operations from Hell and he could talk again, he looked at me and said, "Are you alive? Are we still alive? Because it felt like they were literally killing us!" Later on, when I had my tooth examined in Switzerland, the dentist peered in amazement at the "treatment" I had received at the Nazis' hands. He did his best to repair the job, but the pain will never go away.

That was the German way. Even when they did you a favor, they made sure that the accompanying pain would ensure that you remembered what they had done for as long as you lived. I would never forget that Nazi dentist's appointment, that much was certain. I had seven pieces of tooth to remember it by.

———✦———

Now, just because we were protected citizens in Bergen-Belsen didn't mean that we got to miss out completely on the camp experience. One thing that was the same in every concentration camp was the roll call/head count that took place every morning and every night.

The Germans were obsessed with details. They counted for fun. And if they misplaced even one person, the counting would start all over again. They did this winter and summer. They'd make us stand outside in the early morning, after a night of snow, when the cold was so intense you could get frostbitten in minutes, and then they'd start to count.

One day, I got sick.

I found out later that I'd come down with rheumatic fever. At times my fever was so high that I was delirious, yet life went on and people still needed to be counted. But I could barely walk, and I certainly couldn't stand for hours in the freezing cold. The snow was knee deep and my ankle-height shoes did not provide sufficient protection. To make matters worse, the soles of the shoes were almost completely gone, having thinned out as time wore on. So standing in the snow was true torture.

I felt like a human icicle. Try standing with no shoes and socks in knee-deep snow for a couple of hours every day and night—while raging with fever—and you'll see what I mean.

One day, when the fever was strong and had whittled away at my defenses, I gave in to the pain and told my sister that I couldn't possibly go out for roll call that morning. I was lying on the bed as if all the life had been drained from my tired soul. I no longer cared about the consequences.

A Hungarian woman approached me. She wore a *sheitel*. A religious woman.

"What's the matter? Why isn't she going outside?" she asked those still in the barracks.

"She can't go outside because she doesn't have shoes and the snow is so deep."

"My daughter has an extra pair of shoes." She gave me her daughter's extra pair, and after putting them on, I left the barrack and went out to join the rest of the inmates. But I noticed that her daughter wasn't there.

When I returned from roll call, I saw her daughter lying in bed. The mother had obviously thought that giving me the shoes would serve as an excuse for her daughter's absence, were the Germans to realize she wasn't there. The Hungarians still didn't believe us Polish Jews when we told them stories about the cruelty we had witnessed. Even here in Bergen-Belsen, she still persisted in fondly imagining that the Germans were cultured people who wouldn't hurt a child.

I had hoped that she would lend me the shoes to wear on an ongoing basis, but no such luck. She wanted them back immediately. I needed those shoes. She had an extra pair. Why wouldn't she lend them to me? I will never understand.

CHAPTER 15

I SURVIVED THOSE LAST FEW MONTHS UNDER German authority by an extremely narrow margin.

I wanted the nightmare to be over already. I wanted the suffering to end. I wanted to be reunited with Rivka and my parents and my Zeide Shaya'le. Instead, every day I faced the terrible grayness of Bergen-Belsen, with its constant stench of death.

But for some unknown reason, the Germans intended to keep their promise this time. We were finally informed that it was time for us to commence the next stage of our journey. I was still darkly telling everyone who would listen that I didn't trust the Nazis and that they were going to kill us right before they set us free, but nobody took me seriously.

We chugged along the tracks in the direction of the German/Swiss frontier. I sat at a window and watched in silence as we passed some of the world's most breathtaking scenery. We arrived at a station, where our train was diverted with a series of clanking noises onto Swiss-based tracks. Within minutes we were heading in the direction of the border, and the distant mountains whose snow-covered peaks were enchanting even from afar.

And then, all of a sudden, we were at the border itself. I sat tensely in my seat, imagining the Germans laughing at this, the last possible second, about how they had fooled us. This was when they would order us to get off the train, because they were going to shoot us in the snow.

But that didn't happen.

The train was allowed across the border.

We had just been granted entry to another country. It was a miracle! For the first time since the war began, we were free and safe.

I, however, did not believe that we were truly safe until we arrived at the city of St. Gallen on the Swiss/German border. The capital of the Canton of St. Gallen in Switzerland, the city functions as the gateway to the Appenzal Alps and is a wonderful place to stay if you are going on a skiing vacation.

Which we definitely were not.

But at long last, I was able to relax. When I looked at the Alpine scenery, at the homes perched on the craggy mountainsides, the spotless streets and distinctive architecture, the snow and the peaks and the strangers who spoke so politely, I suddenly realized that I had truly been transported over the border to a new world. A world where nobody was going to shoot at me as if I were an animal being hunted down. As I grasped the magnitude of what had just occurred, I felt a tremendous tension leave my body. I was filled with an overpowering joy that left me literally breathless.

We alighted at the station and were marched in a group to some government offices so we could be registered. The air smelled of freedom. Then I caught sight of some Swiss soldiers, and my fears resurfaced immediately. I couldn't yet tell the difference between a Nazi soldier and a Swiss one. A soldier was a soldier in my book.

There was a crowd of people waiting to greet us. Waving. Overjoyed to see us. Balloons and streamers. It was like a party. They were our brothers, the Jews of Switzerland, and they were waiting at the station to welcome our train into their country.

I'll never forget that welcome. A true "*shalom aleichem.*" I hadn't heard "*Baruch Haba*" being sung in so long! The feelings those words evoked cannot be described.

We were brought to a large school building, with airy classrooms and lots of light. One of the women on the train (Mrs. Schwartz) wasted no time requesting a pair of shoes for me. I received them that same day: a beautiful pair of ski-shoes.

We were bathed. We were taken care of. Given delicious food provided by the Jewish community. The paperwork was dispatched in most efficient Swiss fashion. It was as if we had gone from Hell to Heaven in minutes. It was like a dream come true. Like being transported from a world of black and white to a world of glorious color.

The train brought us into Zurich, where a crowd was waiting to greet the Satmar Rebbe. Imagine that—a group of openly religious Jews standing unashamed and unafraid, ready to pay homage to a great leader. They looked at all of us, and we called out our names. "We're Halberstam, Halberstam —!" And the people knew who we were. Knew Zeide Shaya'le. Knew my great-grandfather, the Divrei Chaim. In a sense, it was a real homecoming for us.

People came rushing to the window of our carriage from all over the platform. They wanted to see the great- grandchildren of the Divrei Chaim. They had so many questions for us. There they stood, those prominent-looking Jews in their luxurious fur coats and lustrous white beards, and the women, so well groomed and fulfilled with concern for us. They stroked our faces and patted our cheeks and had so much to say to us. They wanted to know everything, all at once.

What happened to this one and that one?

Which of our family members were still alive?

Zeide Shaya'le?

This relative, that relative. They wanted to know about the Bochnia ghetto and what was really going on in Klausenberg and Budapest and Satmar. We tried to answer their questions to the best of our ability. They were so thrilled to see us. And we felt alive again for the first time in such a long, long while.

I had been on the run, without anyone to care for me. Now, suddenly, everyone cared.

We cried. But for once, they were tears of happiness.

Our greeters handed us chocolates through the train window, delicious Swiss chocolates, as many as we wanted. And, in my mind, I remembered a little girl named Rivka who turned down the one tiny chocolate I had procured for her, because she was already starving to death and it was pointless for her to eat it. What wouldn't I have given for her to have been there on the train with me, enjoying those chocolates along with the rest of us? Poor Rivka, if she could have just made it through with us — If only she could have been there when we became human beings again.

Life had suddenly become a happy thing once more. One day we were dying a slow death in Bergen-Belsen, and the next we were driving into the municipality of Montreux, known as the Riviera-Pays-d'Enhaut, located in the Canton of Vaud. The city itself is perched on the banks of Lake Geneva, right at the foot of the Alps, and is probably one of the most beautiful places on earth. When you breathe in deeply, you can smell winter and sledding and skiing and riding in a horse-drawn buggy down a mountain with a pack of friends. Tourists stream to this city from around the world to enjoy the natural beauty and sightseeing. Even in those days, this was a tremendously popular destination.

There are castles galore in this part of the country. Some, such as the Cretes Castle, the Chatelard Castle, and Hotel des Alpes, are famous even today. But even back then there were many grand hotels and we were transported to two of them, where we were checked into delightful rooms with views of the nearby mountains and snowy trails. The hotels were fairly empty because there was a war going on and most people weren't taking vacations. But even then some people still came to enjoy the pleasures of the Swiss Alps wonderland.

I loved to open my bedroom window and stick my head out into the freezing air. There was so much to see. Skiers in their brightly colored jerseys heading up the slopes with skis in their hands and backpacks on their backs, ready for a day in the snow. People skating on the frozen lakes. Children romping everywhere with their sleds. And the smell of delicious food and fresh pastries. Switzerland was something else. How nice to be neutral —

Not everything was rosy. My sister was sick. Her kidneys weren't working as well as they should. Even here in Switzerland, her trials continued, and she quickly found herself taken to a hospital. At least we didn't have to worry that the doctors were going to try and kill her there.

While she was in the hospital, the Red Cross took the children on day trips. We got to enjoy the scenery from close up. Mrs. Schwartz looked after us as well. Within a very short time, we had gone from being orphans who no one cared about to children whom everyone wanted to care for.

A few days later, we were taken outside by our Red Cross caretakers, who thoughtfully provided us with child-sized skis that we used to our great delight. Slipping, sliding, and laughing, our minds and emotions free of stress after years of suffering, we were having the time of our lives. I wasn't able to enjoy myself as much as the other members of my group because every time I thought of my sister, my spirits plummeted. She had been sick in Germany (the same kidney ailment) before we got out, and her condition had worsened on our arrival in Switzerland.

How could I enjoy myself in a lighthearted way when my sister was ill?

Being that I was so much younger than she was, our relationship was more like that of mother and child than sisters. She did everything for the four of us. She loved and took care of us. As for my brothers, she'd literally saved their lives. Her illness turned what would have been a lighthearted transition into something a few shades darker. Behind everything I did lurked my worry over her welfare.

Eventually, we were all moved into an orphanage in the city of Vevey. The orphanage had housed a school before the war, catering mainly to Belgium and Dutch children, but those youngsters were long gone and the facility lay open for our use. It was like camp in a way. Vevey itself was a wonderfully calm town, with long, tree-lined boulevards filled with mothers wheeling carriages and people out with their dogs. Nestled in the foothills of the nearby mountains, it was a delightful place to live and we loved it there. Madame Goldberg, a professional camp director, was in charge of our daily programming. She demonstrated that life had much to offer us, even though we were scarred refugees with pasts that made it difficult for us to sleep at night.

Vevey itself is small enough to let a person wander the town on foot, and we did, enjoying the ancient architecture and the pastoral setting. The people were nice to us, our "camp" was incredible, and my sister was getting better. My life had markedly improved in just a short time. We had chores and responsibilities, and lessons to study. We learned together in one group, no matter our age, with the younger students being given the same opportunities as the older ones because our collective focus was to learn as much as we possibly could. Our lives had been interrupted in the absolute worst way imaginable. It was time to try and make up for all of the lost years.

There were special times when we left Vevey as well. Switzerland was home to many Chassidim of Reb Shaya'le and the Divrei Chaim, and when Yom Tov arrived, or even a *Shabbos Hisachdus*, we were always invited to come stay with those who had been supporters of our ancestors in years gone by.

This was right at the end of the war. The Chassidim of Europe had undergone so much suffering. The fact that they were able to gather together for a *Shabbos Hisachdus* was so incredibly joyous that the sheer wonder of it all didn't escape a single person there. I cannot even begin to describe the singing and dancing at a *Yom Tov* celebration, at a *bris*, a bar mitzvah, or a wedding.

The joy of the survivors merged with their guilt — the complex emotions of those who remained alive while everyone around them perished. Every emotion was rich. When we were happy, we were supremely happy. Our sadness had no end. We were survivors, emotionally bereft and yet, at the same time, curiously empowered because of what we had experienced.

The Eisen family took my brothers in on every occasion. I myself had the privilege of spending time with the Fruchthandler family. Rabbi Fruchthandler had gone to *cheder* with my own father and remembered him fondly. My sister had families that treated her as their own as well. We loved the families that took us in and were all the more grateful to them because we already knew that our entire immediate family had been murdered by the Nazi killers. It was just us, the four survivors. Us against the world.

As time passed, we began chafing at the bit. We realized that there was no future for us in Switzerland and we felt that the time had come to move on. And so, after remaining at the orphanage in Vevey for about a year and a half, we finally left Switzerland. Our destination: America.

We arrived in the United States on May 8, 1946.

AMERICA

Chapter Sixteen

W E TRAVELED TO THE UNITED STATES BY
ship. It seemed as though everyone in the world
wanted to get into the United States, and we were
lucky enough to receive the documents necessary to turn
our dream into a reality. I'd sit on a lounge chair on the deck
of the ship, stare out at the faraway horizon, and imagine
where my life was going to take me.

I'd been robbed of my childhood by the chaos and tragedy of war, but my life was still just beginning. I was a young
teenager and had experienced so much already.

I had lived in Sucha and Cracow, run for my life from
Bregal to Bochnia and back again, evading the Nazi's net
time after time. I'd been hunted by men with guns and hidden inside haystacks in the middle of Polish fields. I'd been
soaked by a drenching rain beside my sister and tried to
comfort my Zeide as he cried the tears of a man who knows
what lies in store for him and his fellow Jews in the near
future.

I had confronted the Angel of Death on numerous occasions, and lived to tell the tale. Fore-Maruchki had ordered his own soldiers to make sure I boarded the train safe and sound, and I'd made friends with two Nazi soldiers who protected and vouched for me.

From Poland to Czechoslovakia and into the forests along the border. Klausenberg, Budapest, harrowing train rides, and jumping off trains — I had seen it all. What lay ahead? What would America be like? Were the streets literally paved with gold, like everyone said? While I didn't actually believe that, I assumed there had to be some truth to it if everyone was saying the same thing.

The ocean treated us to a nice, comfortable voyage. There were no storms along the way to throw me out of bed and make my heart pound with fear. We had been through a cruel war but were entering the New World, and our new lives, peacefully.

The ocean was a new experience for a girl who had lived in cities and villages all her life. Endless expanses of water filled my vision from early morning until late at night. Blue. So blue. Sometimes the sky turned a somber gray, and then I'd turn introspective and maudlin, remembering all the things I used to have and would never have again.

Zeide Shaya'le was never far from my mind. I'd recall his shuffling gait, his tender caress on my cheek, his loving remarks and looks.

My parents. My father, waiting at the gate in the Bochnia ghetto, never knowing why his daughter didn't arrive with the loaf of bread she was supposed to bring him.

My mother, the businesswoman, the one who cared about everyone. Whose young daughter died in her arms, and who met her own death while I was far away.

They were always on my mind and in my heart. And yet, I still had two brothers and one sister. I was not alone.

So many others were worse off than I. And we were finally leaving the blood-drenched shores of Europe behind and entering the free world.

It was the greatest feeling anyone could ever have.

<hr/>

The water was no longer blue as our gigantic ship pulled into the harbor at New York. It was a charcoal color, and there were depths to it that frightened me. But the regal statue we encountered with outstretched arm, torch, and crown gave a new meaning to the word freedom.

After that, events speeded up. Before we knew it we found ourselves riding down Stanton Street on the Lower East Side of New York City, searching for the home of our uncle, Reb Chaim'l Tchetchov. He had offered to take us in, and asked for nothing more than to be allowed to raise us and love us as his very own children. After all this time, we were to be reunited with close family again.

My uncle and aunt had had two married children who had been murdered in the war, but they had plenty of room in their hearts for their long-lost relatives. They rented a few small apartments in the building so that we could all settle in comfortably. Another cousin, their grandchild, had survived the war as well; he moved into the building, too. My brothers had a bedroom all to themselves, as did my sister and I. Incredibly as it may seem, we had become children of America.

My uncle loved us with all his heart and soul. He could not do enough for us. He loved us the way he'd loved his own children. He had managed to save a grandchild as well, Mendel'le Halberstam, and he treated the five of us with a powerful devotion. When there was a wedding in the family, he wouldn't agree to attend unless my younger brothers were personally invited to go along with him. The whole family knew that if you wanted to invite the Tchetchov Rav to a *simchah*, you had to include the boys as well. If the boys weren't invited, he took it extremely seriously—almost as if his own brother, my father, hadn't been invited.

Not only was he incredibly devoted to each of us, he also gave the four of us and his grandson ownership of the *sefer* **Divrei Chaim,** which he'd received as an inheritance from Zeide Shaya'le. He wanted us to have it. It had been out of print for years, but eventually my cousin gave the Bobover Chassidim permission to reprint it, which they did.

My sister attended Brooklyn College in the evenings, as part of a program the college was running to teach war refugees English, and she worked at whatever jobs she managed to find during the day. At one point, she assisted Reb Tuvia Halberstam in his capacity as director of Kollel Reb Meir Baal Haneis in the States.

While she was busy working and acclimating, I was trying to find my feet in my new high school on Grand Street. The school had a predominantly Jewish and Italian student body. We got along very nicely with everyone. Life was good: relaxing, calm, even beautiful. And it served its purpose. Those postwar years gave me back my equilibrium and showed me that there was much I could still do in life. I was living in my uncle's home, surrounded by the family and the affection that had been denied us for so long. I was happy.

But inside my heart I knew that my stay in the States was a temporary one. Sooner or later, I would be moving across the ocean to the land of my dreams: Eretz Yisrael. I wasn't sure what my life would be like when I got there, or what kind of future awaited me — but I knew that this was something I had to do. I was determined to make this dream come true. I wanted to live in the land that Zeide Shaya'le hadn't merited to reach, and which the Divrei Chaim had spoken of with such passion. I wanted to reside in the holiest place in the world.

———◦———

And so, I left America with its free and easy ways, with its relaxed people and the promise of a life of financial prosperity, and started out for the Holy Land

This meant taking another ship across a turbulent ocean. It also meant parting from my brothers and sister, with whom I was extremely close. But they would come to visit, and I would visit them. Of that I had no doubt. Once again I was traveling, fulfilling the destiny of one who would constantly move around in life. This had been my lot from the moment of birth (having been born on a train, if you recall), and it had not ended yet.

I didn't have much in the way of earthly belongings. Just a few suitcases and boxes, that was all. My siblings accompanied me to the dock, and we stood together until it was time to say goodbye. Parting from my family was an extremely difficult thing to do. We had barely survived the war. There were so few of us left now, and I was breaking up the remainder. We hugged each other fiercely, and I gazed at their beloved faces through a blur of tears. There came the blast of a giant horn and I had to turn away to climb the gangway.

I stood on the deck and watched my family becoming smaller and smaller, as the enormous ship moved slowly out to sea, the oily water below hinting at an unexplored world that lay beneath. It wasn't long before I couldn't see them anymore. Soon I couldn't see land anymore either.

It was 1949, and I was on my way to the port at Haifa.

The next few days were filled with the bittersweet feelings our parting had evoked. On the one hand, I was incredibly excited about my imminent arrival in Eretz Yisrael. On the other hand, I couldn't help but cry every time I remembered that I had left my little brothers behind on the shores of America. The sea was usually calm, though that could change without warning. But the journey proved to be an easy one, and soon enough we were approaching Haifa and my future home.

Today, a huge number of Jews make the decision to live in Israel. And they come by plane to a brand-new airport. It was very different for me. I stepped off the gangway in the port of Haifa and onto the wonderful earth of my new home. Every step was a pleasure. Every glimpse of that deliciously blue Mediterranean Sea sent a shiver up my spine. Had I really just crossed that huge expanse all on my own?

Apparently so.

I was all set to begin my brand-new life—combining the memories of my past with the hopes for my future. I was confident and secure, buoyed by the tender blessings of Zeide Shaya'le and the knowledge of who I was and where I came from.

With my head held high and smiling from deep within, I strode toward my new life, thankful that I had been granted the opportunity to start afresh, and intent on fulfilling my destiny.

CHAPTER SEVENTEEN

WHEN I ARRIVED IN ERETZ YISRAEL, MOST of the people around me were single. As the years marched on, *shidduchim* were being made on a regular basis. It seemed as if every day we were hearing about another couple that had become engaged. And the weddings — they were so beautiful.

Picture the scene.

Everyone bedecked in their finest clothing, as befit a wedding celebration. A *chuppah* is set up on the great open area in front of a *shul*. And then the sound of a lone violin heralds the approach of the *chassan*, escorted by two close friends (almost never a parent; that was too much to expect back then). We'd watch with tears in our eyes.

The sun would be beginning its descent into the earth. A red-orange halo ushered the *kallah* towards the *chuppah* where her future husband awaited. And, as we watched, our minds would be drawn against our will to a place across the ocean where so many of our relatives had been lost. Auschwitz. Bergen-Belsen. Treblinka. Majdanek. The slaughtering ground of Poland and Germany. Our mothers and fathers, Zeide Shaya'le. All smiling and at peace now. Overjoyed that we were still *Yidden* above all. Still wanting nothing more than to carry out the will of *Hashem*.

And the Rav would perform the marriage ceremony, and the sound of Amen! would ring out through the nighttime air. And then the celebration would begin—the joy, the festivity, the sheer, unbridled merriment and absolute ecstasy of those simple moments.

With *Hashem's* help we had survived.

First Europe.

Now the Arabs.

And we were on our way to rebuilding the Jewish families that had been lost to us in the ashes of Europe. Those were true celebrations. This was genuine joy.

I remember one occasion in particular. It stands out in my memory because it was a double wedding. Two Argentinean couples were married on the same night. Rav Aryeh Levine came from Jerusalem to officiate. I'll never forget the sight of him standing under the *chuppah*, a glass of wine in his hand, the light reflecting off his lustrous beard, and tears streaming down his face.

"I never thought I'd live to see so many of you getting married."

He'd seen these people suffer under the British. He'd adopted some of them while they were still in prison. And now he was standing with his "children" as they prepared to build a *bayis ne'eman b'Yisrael*. The moment cannot really be described. Except to say that this was true happiness.

———⊷•⊶———

My husband's name was Yaakov (Jacobo) Preiser. He hailed originally from South America. Yaakov was quiet, calm, and intelligent. Never hurried. Never angry. A perfect gentleman.

He knew so much about everything. He was such a treasure trove of information that he had been nicknamed "the walking encyclopedia." He was always writing articles in his native Spanish for the people back home. Yaakov was the kind of man who never fought with anyone. A true peacemaker, with a beautiful sense of humor. He had not an enemy in the world. And he was a *Kohen*.

Yaakov came from an observant and upstanding family. His father was one of the individuals who'd established the local *Chevra Kaddisha* back in Argentina, despite being a *Kohen* and therefore not allowed to actively participate in burying the dead. Yaakov grew up watching his parents sacrificing for *Yiddishkeit* on a daily basis.

Torah study was important enough to his parents that they made sure to hire a private *melamed* to teach Yaakov in his own home. And when we came to visit his family in Argentina, I would see his Uncle Mordechai sitting for hours at a time hunched over his Gemara, learning with a fire and an intensity that I hadn't witnessed since my days in Sucha, first at Zeide Shaya'le's court and later on in my Uncle Chaim's home. They were a family that cared about Torah and for whom Judaism was a priority, and that was what I wanted for myself.

———⊰•⊱———

It was 1954, and we were getting married. Our engagement lasted about eight months. We were waiting for the *chassan's* parents to arrive and it took that long to arrange their trip.

Our wedding was a day I will never forget. Here I was, an orphan girl plucked from the flames of Europe, about to begin building my own *bayis ne'eman b'Yisrael*—with a wonderful man who would be my life's partner. Who would ever have imagined such an outcome?

I sat in a regal white chair, garbed in my wedding gown. Crowds of friends surrounded me on all sides. I sat there praying fervently for the future—and for the past. Memories assailed me then, as they do to this day. (You can never really escape the war. The most you can hope for is to not to think about it too often. Even now, I sometimes wake up in the middle of the night from the nightmares and the pain of those bitter memories.)

Though I was physically sitting in Eretz Yisrael, my mind was full of pictures of a time not so long before, when every day had felt as if it would be my last.

Sucha. The tar pit. Hiding in the chicken coops.

Bregal and Bochnia. Sickness and people dying in the streets.

The icy rain that killed my sister. My poor Rivka, wasting away in front of me. Skin and bones.

(I still cry when I think of her.)

Hiding from the Nazis.

The commandant using me for target practice in the ghetto streets. Shooting at the terror-stricken "rabbit."

Arrested in the train station. The metallic taste of fear as the soldier called Fore-Maruchki on the telephone.

Trying to bring my father bread, and failing.

The tears run down my cheeks.

Hiding in the dug-out haystack.

Zeide Shaya'le's tears. Pure tears from such pure eyes. Rain washing the windows of that little room in Bochnia on Tishah B'Av night.

Zeide, how I love you. How I miss you still! You were the most precious, the most beautiful, sweetest Zeide in the world. How you loved us! With an angelic love —

Crossing the borders. Over mountains. Through rivers.

Surviving on nothing for days and days. Struggling to keep the children who were with me quiet so we wouldn't get caught.

So many narrow escapes. So many miraculous moments.

My time in prison. Sleeping in a cell for weeks on end.

Escaping the shochet's house just in time.

The wagon, pulling up in the exact window of time before the patrol entered the yard.

Taking a seat in the train's front carriage. The one with the Nazi soldiers.

Becoming friends with them. Singing songs. Making animal sounds. The Hungarian officers approaching.

Laying my head in the soldier's lap!!!

Hashem taking me by the hand, every single time.

Jumping from the train.

Event after event rushed through my mind. My thoughts raced in time to my beating heart.

I'm getting married. So many aren't here with me on this awe-inspiring day. Mama. Tatte. Zeide Shaya'le. My brothers and sisters. They are watching me from heaven. They are here in spirit.

Then the music started to play, and Yaakov was coming. It was time for the *badeken*. Time to begin the next portion of my life.

I will never forget you, I promised them all silently.

And then it was time to stand up and walk to the *chuppah*.

———◦———

Malka Yakobovitch, younger sister of Reb Shloime Halberstam (the Bobover Rebbe), with whom I was very close, walked me down to the *chuppah*. Another sister, Rivchu, who was also my aunt, attended my wedding as well.

A *shochet* butchered a sheep in honor of our big day, and

since the wedding took place during the grape harvest, there were clusters of succulent grapes everywhere. In fact, if I close my eyes today, I can still smell the heady aroma of the festive tables covered in color, the ripe grapes leaking juice all over the tablecloths. The fruits of Eretz Yisrael.

EPILOGUE

I WAS MARRIED TO MY HUSBAND FOR FIFTY-THREE blessed years. We were blessed with three children, two born in Eretz Yisrael and one in the United States. I watched them grow up. Sometimes, they were healthy; many times, they were not. I stayed up nights and held their little hands and wiped the sweat from their brows and reassured myself that if we had come this far, *Hashem* wouldn't abandon us now.

Three children.

A boy named Yonatan.

A boy named Uriel.

And a girl named Haya.

Uriel lives in Eretz Yisrael, as I do.

Yonatan and Haya live in the States.

I have had a long life. There has been a great deal of traveling, very much in the spirit of someone who was born on a train.

I have traveled to South America with my husband and learned Spanish. I later used this language when I taught immigrant children in the States.

I have lived in Europe, the United States, Eretz Yisrael, and Argentina. I have moved back and forth between Eretz Yisrael and America, and now I am living in Eretz Israel, where my dear Yaakov is buried. Along the way, I learned many different languages and dialects and much about all kinds of people, how they think and what makes them who they are. I have led an interesting life filled with memories of my grandfather and stories of my great-grandfather and the love and precious beauty of strong family connections.

I see my grandchildren and great-grandchildren. Some I don't get to see as often as I would like, but I love every single one of them.

Sometimes I still can't believe all the things that happened to me in the course of my life. The war — such a crazy, terrifying adventure. Living in Israel after the war —

I have been blessed with so much good in my life, so many blessings. And I thank *Hashem* for granting me all His bountiful kindness year after year and decade after decade. My children are wonderful and have built beautiful families. I dearly love each and every one of them. When I'm in Israel, I miss the ones in the States; when I'm in the States, I miss the ones in Eretz Yisrael. I was blessed with a wonderful, loving, patient, and intelligent husband who treated me like a queen.

And I was blessed with a Zeide Shaya'le, who knew that I would survive and whose memory is always with me. And who taught me that when we are crying here on earth, the Heavens cry great tears of sorrow as well.

The End

GLOSSARY

agunah — woman who cannot remarry because (a) her husband cannot or will not give her a divorce, or (b) it cannot be verified whether he is still alive.

aktion (German) —any non-military campaign to further Nazi ideals of race, but most often referred to the assembly and deportation of Jews to concentration or death camps.

al kiddush Hashem — acting for the sake of bringing honor to Hashem; acting for the sake of the sanctification of G-d's Name.

aleph-beis — Hebrew alphabet.

aliyah, aliyos — lit., going up. 1. spiritual uplift. 2. the act of being called to recite a blessing at the public reading of the Torah. 3. immigration to Israel.

am ha'aretz — an ignorant Jew; as a result he may not be meticulous in his observance of some aspects of Jewish law.

Asher Yatzar — prayer said after performing bodily functions.

Ashrecha! — How fortunate you are!

Avinu — lit., our father, usually used in reference to the Patriarchs.

avodah zarah — idolatry.

b'ezras Hashem — with G-d's help

badeken — (Yiddish) the part of the wedding at which the bride's face is veiled prior to being escorted to the *chuppah*.

Baruch Haba — lit., blessed be the one who has arrived; words of welcome.

bayis ne'eman b'Yisrael — lit., a worthy house in Israel; a blessing to establish a Torah-true home, generally referring to a bride and groom.

Beis Din (pl. *Batei Din*) — rabbinic court.

Beis Midrash — study hall where Torah is learned.

bekishe — long black coat, typically made of silk and worn by some Chassidic Jews.

bentch gomel — recite a blessing thanking Hashem for rescuing one from a dangerous situation.

berachah (pl. *berachos*) – 1. blessing. 2. expression of goodwill and blessings for success bestowed by a Chasidic Rebbe.

blech — (Yiddish) a sheet of metal placed over a stovetop above the flame to permit keeping the Shabbos food over the fire.

chas v'shalom — Heaven forbid.

chasunah (pl. *chasunos*) — wedding.

chavrusa (pl. *chavrusos*) — study partner.

chazzan — cantor.

cheder — school, usu. an elementary school (spec. for Jewish studies).

cheirem — excommunication.

chesed — lovingkindness; acts of benevolence.

Chevra Kaddisha — Jewish burial society.

chillul Hashem — desecration of G-d's Name.

chinuch — Jewish education; Torah education (of minors).

Chumash — one of the Five Books of the Torah; the Five Books collectively.

chuppah — 1. wedding canopy. 2. the marriage ceremony.

churban — 1. destruction. 2. (cap.) destruction of the Holy Temple. 3. the Holocaust.

d'veikus — bonding with or clinging to God.

daven — (Yiddish) to pray.

dayan (pl. *dayanim*) — halachic decisor or judge.

Der Zeide — (Yiddish) lit., "the grandfather"; a formal or respectful way to refer to a grandfather

derashah — lecture, esp. a lecture on a Torah topic.

derech eretz — proper conduct; respect; courtesy.

din Torah — 1. case brought to a halachic court. 2. decision rendered by a halachic court.

ehrlichkeit — (Yiddish) honesty.

eineklach (sing. *einikel*) — grandchildren

Eliyahu HaNavi — Elijah the Prophet; tradition has it that he comes to the aid of people in dire situations

elter zeide — (Yiddish) great-grandfather.

emunah — faith; belief in G-d.

eruv, eruvin — lit., to combine; to mix together; here, domain(s).

Ezras Nashim — women's section of a *shul*.

frum — (Yiddish) religious; Torah observant.

gabbai (pl. *gabbaim*) — synagogue sexton; attendant of a Chassidic Rebbe; person responsible for the proper functioning of a synagogue or other communal body.

gadol (pl. *gedolim*) — outstanding Torah scholar; a man of greatness; lit., great; a term used to refer to a person of great stature; a saintly individual.

galuchim — non-Jewish priests.

get — divorce; bill of divorce.

Hakadosh Baruch Hu — lit., the Holy One (i.e., Hashem), Blessed Is He; G-d.

hakaras hatov — gratitude.

Hashem — G-d.

Hashem yikom damam — "may G-d avenge their blood."

hashgachah — Divine oversight. Hashgachah; Hashem's involvement in every aspect of existence.

hashkafah (pl. *hashkafos*) — outlook; ideology; worldview; a concept of *emunah*.

Havdalah — lit., separation; the prayer said to end the Sabbath or Festival, differentiating between holy and secular.

heilige — (Yiddish) holy.

heilige Yidden — (Yiddish) holy Jews.

kallah — a bride; girl who is engaged to be married.

kehillah — congregation; community.

kinderlach — (Yiddish) affectionate term for children.

Kinnos — book of elegies read on the Ninth of Av.

Klal Yisrael — Jewish people in general; the community of Israel; the entire Jewish community, taken as a single entity.

klap — (Yiddish) a blow; a clap.

Kohen (pl. *Kohanim*) — member of the priestly family descended in the male line from Aaron.

korban (pl. *korbanos*) — sacrificial offering.

l'chaim — 1. party celebrating an engagement. 2. toast over a drink of wine or whiskey.

l'chavod — in honor of.

lamdan (pl. *lamdanim*) — 1. teacher of Jewish studies. 2. Talmudic scholar.

lashon hara — lit., evil speech; derogatory speech; slander.

letcho (Hungarian) — dish usually consisting of sautéed onions, peppers, tomatoes, and mushrooms.

lomdish — (Yiddish) learned, complicated.

lukshen — (Yiddish) egg noodles.

Maariv — evening prayer service.

malach — angel.

Malach Hamaves — Angel of Death.

mazal — luck; fortune.

melamed (pl. *melamdim*) — teacher, esp. of young children.

mentsch (pl. *mentschen*) — (Yiddish) lit., man; connotes a man or woman who exemplifies integrity, respect, and kindness.

meshugene — one who is insane or who behaves irrationally.

mesirus nefesh — selfless devotion, even to the extent that one is willing to give one's life to sanctify Hashem's Name.

minhag (pl. *minhagim*) — custom.

minyan (pl. *minyanim*) — quorum of ten men necessary for conducting a prayer service; group for communal prayer service.

mitzvah (pl. *mitzvos*) — good deed; one of the 613 commandments; Biblical or Rabbinic commandment.

Mizrach vant — (Yiddish) eastern wall in a synagogue.

Modeh Ani — lit., "I admit in front of You"; prayer recited upon awakening in the morning, expressing gratitude for life.

mofeis — lit., proof used to describe a miracle or miraculous occurence.

moser nefesh — to be self-sacrificing; to exhibit total and unlimited devotion.

Motza'ei Shabbos — Saturday night; the time of the departure of the Sabbath.

navi — prophet.

neshamah (pl. *neshamos*) — soul.

niftar — (n.) deceased person. (v.) died.

"Nine Days" — the nine days beginning wih Rosh Chodesh Av, culminating in the fast of the Ninth of Av.

Olam HaBa — the World to Come; a designation for the eternal afterlife.

Olam HaEmes — lit., the World of Truth; the Next World.

pasuk (pl. *pesukim*) — verse in the Tanach or liturgy.

pengo — (Hungarian) unit of Hungarian currency.

Pesach — Passover.

peyos — earlocks; side curls.

pilpul — 1. sophistry. 2. hair-splitting Talmudic debate; penetrating Talmudic investigation. 3. disputation and drawing of conclusions.

psak — halachic decision.

Ribbono shel Olam — lit., Master of the World; Hashem.

ruach hakodesh — Divine spirit or inspiration.

schnell — (German) quickly, fast.

seder (pl. *sedarim*) — 1. study period. 2. study session. 3. u.c., Pesach-night ritual during which the Haggadah is recited. 4. set time, usually for learning. 5. any of the six Orders of the Mishnah.

sefer (pl. *sefarim*) — book, specifically a book on holy subjects ; book, esp. on a learned topic.

Sefirah — the counting of the seven weeks from the second day of Passover until Shavuos.

sha — (Yiddish) (interjection) be quiet; be still.

Shabbos Hisachdus — Chassidic gathering of unity taking place throughout Shabbos.

Shalom aleichem — lit., peace be on you; traditional greeting; Friday-evening song of welcome to the ministering angels.

shamash — synagogue attendant, sexton; personal assistant.

Shavuos — Pentecost; the festival that commemorates the giving of the Torah.

sheitel (Yiddish) — wig.

Shema Yisrael — abbreviated term for "*Shema Yisrael, Hashem Elokeinu, Hashem Echad!* — Hear O Israel,

Hashem is our God, Hashem is the One and Only"; this prayer, recited twice daily, expresses the essence of Jewish faith.

shivah — seven-day mourning period immediately following the death of a close relative.

shochet — ritual slaughterer; one who slaughters an animal in accordance with Jewish/Torah law.

shtetl — (Yiddish) village.

shtiebel (pl. *shtieblach*) — (Yiddish) small synagogue, often situated in a house.

shul — (Yiddish) synagogue; house of prayer.

Simchas Torah — the festival honoring the completion of the yearly cycle of the Torah reading.

siyata d'Shmaya — Divine Providence; help from Hashem.

succah (pl. *succos*) — booth in which Jews are commanded to dwell during Succos.

Succos — Tabernacles; the Festival during which one is commanded to dwell in a *succah*.

tallis (pl. *tallesim*) — prayer shawl; four-cornered prayer shawl with fringes at each corner, worn by (married) men during morning prayers.

talmid chacham (pl. *talmidei chachamim*) — lit., student of a wise person; person learned in Torah and Talmud; Torah scholar.

Talmud Torah — school where Torah subjects are taught.

Tatte — (Yiddish) Father.

Tefillas Haderech — the wayfarer's prayer.

Tehillim — 1. Book of *Psalms*. 2. psalms.

tereifah — nonkosher food.

Tishah B'Av — the ninth day of the month of Av, fast day commemorating the destruction of both the First and Second Temples in Jerusalem.

tzaddik (m.) *tzadeikkes*; (f.) (pl. *tzaddikim*) — righteous person.

tzaros — problems, troubles.

tzidkus — righteousness.

Ushpizin — lit., guests; the seven spiritual guests who visit the succah during the Festival of Succos.

Yad Hashem — Hand of G-d.

yahrtzeit — (Yiddish) the anniversary of a death.

yeshivah — school of Jewish studies; school where Torah is studied; Torah academy.

yetzer hara — evil inclination, connotes the negative impulse to behave contrary to the Torah's commandments.

Yid (pl. *Yidden*) (Yiddish) — Jews.

Yiddishkeit (Yiddish) — Judaism; the Jewish way of life.

Yom Tov (pl. *Yamim Tovim*) — Jewish holiday.

zeeskeit — (Yiddish) sweetie; term of endearment.

zeide (Yiddish) — grandfather.

z'man simchaseinu — time of our rejoicing; refers to the Yom Tov of Succos.